John Neal

Great Mysteries and Little Plagues

John Neal
Great Mysteries and Little Plagues
ISBN/EAN: 9783743350496
Manufactured in Europe, USA, Canada, Australia, Japa
Cover: Foto ©ninafisch / pixelio.de

Manufactured and distributed by brebook publishing software (www.brebook.com)

John Neal

Great Mysteries and Little Plagues

Great Mysteries

AND

Little Plagues.

BY

JOHN NEAL.

BOSTON:
ROBERTS BROTHERS.
1870.

Entered according to Act of Congress, in the year 1869, by
ROBERTS BROTHERS,
In the Clerk's Office of the District Court of the Dist. of Massachusetts.

STEREOTYPED BY REGAN & LEADBEATER,
55 Water Street.

PREFACE.

I HATE prefaces; and the older I grow, the more I hate them, and the more unwilling I am to transgress — in that way — with my eyes open.

But something must be said, I suppose, if only by way of an advertisement, or warning.

When I had finished what one of my daughters persists in calling my "NAUGHTY-BIOGRAPHY," and the other, "PERSONALITIES" — while my hair has grown visibly thinner, I will not say under what kind of domestic remonstrance from another quarter, and a very amiable, though witty somebody writes it "*Maundering* Recollections" — I had an idea that, if I went further, I might be found "painting the lily, gilding refined gold," etc., etc., and so I pulled up — for the present.

But this little book was already under way. I had promised it, and such promises I always keep — and for the best of reasons: I cannot afford to break them.

When I turned out the original of " Children — What are they good for?" some forty years ago, or thereabouts, I had never met with, nor heard of, anything in that way. Children were overlooked. Their droppings were unheeded — out of the nursery. But now, and in fact very soon after my little essay appeared in the "Atlantic Souvenir," if I do not mistake, the papers and magazines, both abroad and at home, were continually brightened up with diamond-sparks and with Down-easterly or "Orient pearls, at random strung," which seemed to have been picked up in play-grounds, or adrift, or along the highway; and itemizers were seen dodging round among the little folks, wherever they were congregated, or following them as the Chinese follow a stranger, if they see him make wry faces.

For amusement only, and to keep myself out of mischief — I hope I have succeeded — just after the fire, not having much to do beyond twirling my thumbs, and trying to whistle "I cares for nobody, and nobody cares for me," I began collecting such as fell in my way.

My first idea was to call them "KINDLING-STUFF," or "OVEN-WOOD," as characteristic, if not of them, at least of the compiler; but finding the collection grew upon me, and myself growing serious, I adopted "PICKINGS AND STEALINGS," which, on the whole, I think still more characteristic, beside being both suggestive and descriptive.

"GOODY GRACIOUS, A FAIRY STORY," I wrote for the purpose of showing — and *proving* — that fairy stories need not be crowded with extravagant impossibilities, to engage the attention of our little folks; and that if they are so contrived as to seem true, or at least possible, they need not be unwholesome. Am I wrong?

And furthermore saith not, as Jacob Barker used to write, at the bottom of his letters,

"Your respected friend,"

J. N.

CONTENTS.

I.—CHILDREN—WHAT ARE THEY GOOD FOR?

II.—GOODY GRACIOUS! AND THE FORGET-ME-NOT.

III.—PICKINGS AND STEALINGS.

CHILDREN—WHAT ARE THEY GOOD FOR?

THE child is father of the man. Men are but children of a larger growth. How often do we meet with this array of words! Yet how insensible we are to the profound philosophy they enwrap. Sublime and astonishing truths! Uttered every day in our hearing, set before our eyes at every step of our journey through life, written over all the monuments of Earth, upon the pages and banners of all History, upon the temples and the pyramids, the palaces and the sepulchres of departed Nations, upon all the doings of the Past and the Present, as with unextinguishable fire, and sounding forever and ever in the unapproachable solitudes of the Future! Yet heard with indifference, read without emotion, and repeated from mouth to mouth, day after day and year after year, without a suspicion of their deep meaning, of their transcendent importance, of their imperishable beauty. And why? The language is too familiar, the apparent signification too simple and natural for the excited understandings of the multitude. There is no curtain to be lifted, no veil to be rent as with the hands of giants, no zone to be loosened, no mystery to be expounded afar off, as in the language of another world, nothing to be guessed at, or deciphered, nothing but what anybody might understand if he would; and, *therefore*, nothing to be remembered or cared for.

But, in simple truth, a more sublime interrogation could not be propounded than that which may appear to be answered by the language referred to. *What are children?*

Step to the window with me. The street is full of them. Yonder a school is let loose; and here, just within reach of our observation, are two or three noisy little fellows; and there another party mustering for play. Some are whispering together, and plotting so loudly and so earnestly, as to attract everybody's attention; while others are holding themselves aloof, with their satchels gaping so as to betray a part of their plans for tomorrow afternoon, or laying their heads together in pairs, for a trip to the islands. Look at them, weigh the question I have put to you, and then answer it, as it deserves to be answered. *What are children?* To which you reply at once, without any sort of hesitation perhaps, — "Just as the twig is bent the tree's inclined"; or, "Men are but children of a larger growth"; or, peradventure, "The child is father of the man." And then, perhaps, you leave me, perfectly satisfied with yourself and with your answer, having "plucked out the heart of the mystery," and uttered, without knowing it, a string of glorious truths, — pearls of great price.

But, instead of answering you as another might, instead of saying, *Very true*, what if I were to call you back to the window with words like these: Do you know what you have said? do you know the meaning of the language you have employed? or, in other words, *do you know your own meaning?* what would you think of me? That I was playing the philosopher, perhaps, that I wanted to puzzle you with a childish question, that I thought I was thinking, or at best that I was a little out of my senses. Yet, if you were a man of understanding, I should have paid you a high compliment; a searcher after truth, I should have done you a great favor;

a statesman, a lawgiver, a philanthropist, a patriot, or a father who deserved to be a father, I should have laid you under everlasting obligations, I should have opened a boundless treasury underneath your feet, I should have translated you instantly to a new world, carried you up into a high mountain, as it were, and set before you all the kingdoms of the earth, with all their revolutions and changes, all future history, the march of armies, the growth of conquerors, the waxing and the waning of empire, the changes of opinion, the apparition of thrones dashing against thrones, the overthrow of systems, and the revolution of ages.

Among the children who are now playing *together*,—like birds among the blossoms of earth, haunting all the green shadowy places thereof, and rejoicing in the bright air; happy and beautiful creatures, and as changeable as happy, with eyes brimful of joy, and with hearts playing upon their little faces like sunshine upon clear waters; among those who are now idling together on that slope, or hunting butterflies together on the edge of that wood, a wilderness of roses, — you would see not only the gifted and the powerful, the wise and the eloquent, the ambitious and the renowned, the long-lived and the long-to-be-lamented of another age, but the wicked and the treacherous, the liar and the thief, the abandoned profligate and the faithless husband, the gambler and the drunkard, the robber, the burglar, the ravisher, the murderer, and the betrayer of his country. *The child is father of the man.*

Among them, and that other little troop just appearing, children with yet happier faces and pleasanter eyes, the blossoms of the future — the mothers of nations — you would see the founders of states and the destroyers of their country, the steadfast and the weak, the judge and the criminal, the murderer and the executioner, the exalted and the lowly, the unfaithful wife and the broken-hearted husband, the proud betrayer and his pale victim, the living and breathing portents and prodigies, the embodied virtues and vices, of another age and of another world, *and all playing together!* Men are but children of a larger growth.

Pursuing the search, you would go forth among the little creatures, as among the types of another and a loftier language, the mystery whereof has been just revealed to you,—a language to become universal hereafter, types in which the autobiography of the Future was written ages and ages ago. Among the innocent and helpless creatures that are called *children*, you would see warriors, with their garments rolled in blood, the spectres of kings and princes, poets with golden harps and illuminated eyes, historians and painters, architects and sculptors, mechanics and merchants, preachers and lawyers; here a grave-digger flying his kite with his future customers, there a physician playing at marbles with his; here the predestined to an early and violent death for cowardice, fighting the battles of a whole neighborhood; there a Cromwell or a Cæsar, a Napoleon or a Washington, hiding themselves for fear, enduring reproach or insult with patience; a Benjamin Franklin higgling for nuts or gingerbread, or the "Old Parr" of another generation sitting apart in the sunshine, and shivering at every breath of wind that reaches him. Yet we are told that "just as the twig is bent, the tree's inclined."

Hereafter is made up of the shreds and patches of Heretofore. If "Men are but children of a larger growth," then *what are children?* Men of a smaller growth. And this happens to be the truth, not only in the world of imagination, but in the world of realities; not only among poets, but among lawyers. At law, children are men, — little children murderers. A boy of nine, and others of ten and eleven, have been put to death in England, two for murder, and a third for "cunningly and maliciously" firing two barns. Of the little murderers, one killed his playmate and the other his bedfellow. One hid the body, and the other himself. And therefore, said the judges, they knew they had done wrong, — they could distinguish between good and evil; and therefore they ordered both to be strangled. And they were strangled accordingly. As if a child who is old enough to know that he has done wrong, is therefore old enough to know that he deserves death!

So with regard to children of the other sex.

At law, babies are women, women babies. The same law which classes our mothers and our wives, our sisters and our daughters, with infants, lunatics, idiots, and "persons beyond sea," allows a child to be betrothed at seven, to be endowed of her future husband's estate at nine, and to agree or disagree to a previous marriage at twelve. And what is law in England is law here. We are still governed by the Court of King's Bench, the lawyers and the judges of Westminister Hall. Let no man say, therefore, that these are the dreams of poetry, the glittering shapes that wander about forever and ever among the vast chambers of a disordered imagination. They are not so. They are no phantasms, — they are realities, they are substantial existences, they "are known to the law."

Such are children. Corrupted, they are fountains of bitterness for ages. Would you plant for the skies? Plant in the live soil of the warm and generous and youthful; pour all your treasures into the hearts of children. Would you look into the future as with the spirit of prophecy, and read as with a telescope the history and character of our country, and of other countries? You have but to watch the eyes of children at play.

What children are, neighborhoods are. What neighborhoods are, communities are,— states, empires, worlds! They are the elements of Hereafter made visible.

Even fathers and mothers look upon children with a strange misapprehension of their dignity. Even with the poets, they are only the flowers and blossoms. the dew-drops, or the playthings of earth. Yet "of such is the kingdom of heaven." The Kingdom of Heaven! with all its principalities and powers, its hierarchies, dominations, thrones! The Saviour understood them better; to Him their true dignity was revealed. Flowers! They are the flowers of the invisible world,—indestructible, self-perpetuating flowers, with each a multitude of angels and evil spirits underneath its leaves, toiling and wrestling for dominion over it! Blossoms! They are the blossoms of another world, whose fruitage is angels and archangels. Or dew-drops? They are dew-drops that have their source, not in the chambers of the earth, nor among the vapors of the sky, which the next breath of wind, or the next flash of sunshine may dry up forever, but among the everlasting fountains and inexhaustible reservoirs of mercy and love. Playthings! God!—if the little creatures would but appear to us in their true shape for a moment! We should fall upon our faces before them, or grow pale with consternation, —or fling them off with horror and loathing.

What would be our feelings to see a fair child start up before us a maniac or a murderer, armed to the teeth? to find a nest of serpents on our pillow? a destroyer, or a traitor, a Harry the Eighth, or a Benedict Arnold asleep in our bosom? A Catherine or a Peter, a Bacon, a Galileo, or a Bentham, a Napoleon or a Voltaire, clambering up our knees after sugar-plums? Cuvier laboring to distinguish a horse-fly from a blue-bottle, or dissecting a spider with a rusty nail? La Place trying to multiply his own apples, or to subtract his playfellow's gingerbread? What should we say to find ourselves romping with Messalina, Swedenborg, and Madame de Stael? or playing bo-peep with Murat, Robespierre, and Charlotte Corday? or puss-puss in the corner with George Washington, Jonathan Wild, Shakspeare, Sappho, Jeremy Taylor, Mrs. Clark, Alfieri, and Harriet Wilson? Yet stranger things have happened. These were all children but the other day, and clambered about the knees, and rummaged in the pockets, and nestled in the laps of people no better than we are. But *if* they had appeared in their true shape for a single moment, while playing together! What a scampering there would have been among the grown folks! How their fingers would have tingled!

Now to me there is no study half so delightful as that of these little creatures, with hearts fresh from the gardens of the sky, in their first and fairest and most unintentional disclosures, while they are indeed a mystery, a fragrant, luminous, and beautiful mystery. And I have an idea that if we only had a name for the study, it might be found as attractive and as popular, and perhaps — though I would not go too far — *perhaps* about as advantageous in the long run to the future fathers and mothers of mankind, as the study of shrubs and flowers, or that of birds and fishes. And why not? They are the cryptogamia of another world, — the infusoria of the skies.

Then why not pursue the study for yourself? The subjects are always before you. No books are needed, no costly drawings, no lectures, neither transparencies nor illustrations. Your specimens are all about you. They come and go at your bidding. They are not to be hunted for, along the edge of a precipice, on the borders of the wilderness, in the desert, nor by the sea-shore. They abound, not in the uninhabited or unvisited place, but in your very dwelling-houses, about the steps of your doors, in every street of every village, in every green field, and every crowded thoroughfare. They flourish bravely in snow-storms, in the dust of the trampled highway, where drums are beating and colors flying — in the roar of cities. They love the sounding sea-breeze and the open air, and may always be found about the wharves, and rejoicing before the windows of toy-shops. They love the blaze of fireworks and the smell of gunpowder; and where that is, they are, to a dead certainty.

You have but to go abroad for half an hour in pleasant weather, or to throw open your doors or windows on a Saturday afternoon, if you live anywhere in the neighborhood of a school-house, or a vacant lot, with here and there a patch of green, or a dry place in it, and steal behind the curtains, or draw the blinds, and let the fresh wind blow through and through the chambers of your heart for a few minutes, winnowing the dust and scattering the cobwebs that have gathered there while you were asleep, and lo! you will find it ringing with the voices of children at play, and all alive with the glimmering phantasmagoria of leap-frog, prison-base, or knock-up-and-catch.

Let us try the experiment. There! I have opened the windows, I have drawn the blinds, and hark! already there is the sound of little voices afar off, like "sweet bells jangling." Nearer and nearer come they, and now we catch a glimpse of bright faces peeping round the corners, and there, by that empty inclosure, you see a general mustering and swarming, as of bees about a newly-discovered flower-garden. But the voices we now hear proceed from two little fellows who have withdrawn from the rest. One carries a large basket, and his eyes are directed to my window; he doesn't half like the blinds being drawn. The other follows him, with a tattered book under his arm, rapping the posts, one after the other, as he goes along. He is clearly on bad terms with himself. And now we can see their faces. Both are grave, and one rather pale, and trying to look ferocious. And hark! now we are able to distinguish their words. "Well, I ain't skeered o' you," says the foremost and the larger boy. "Nor I ain't skeered o' you," retorts the other; "but you needn't say you meant to lick me." And so I thought. Another, less acquainted with children, might not be able to see the connection; but I could, — it was worthy of Aristotle himself, or John Locke. "I *didn't* say I meant to lick ye," rejoined the first, "I said I *could* lick ye, and so I can." To which the other replies, glancing first at my window and then all up and down street, "I should like to see you try." Whereupon the larger boy begins to move away, half backwards, half sideways, muttering just loud enough to be heard, "Ah, you want to fight now, jest 'cause you're close by your own house." And here the dialogue finished, and the babies moved on, shaking their little heads at each other, and muttering all the way up street. Men are but children of a larger growth! Children but Empires in miniature.

How beautiful and how strange are the first combinations of thought in a wayward or peevish child! And then, how alike we all are in our waywardness and peevishness! It is but a change of name, and one trifle is about as good as another to breed a quarrel, or to throw the wisest and the best of our grown babies off their balance. A bit of writing, the loss of a paper with pictures on it, a handful of glittering dust, or somebody making mouths at us, a word or a look, and we are stamping with rage, or miserable for half a day. A cloud coming up when the horses are at the door, a little bad weather, a spot upon our new clothes, or a lump of sugar not quite so large as another's; and what children we are! How perfectly wretched!

I once knew a little boy, who, after sitting awhile as if lost in thought, turned to his mother, and said: "Mother! what did you marry my father for? Why didn't you wait till I grew up, and then marry me?" Rather a strange question, to be sure, and the little fellow was but just old enough to put his words together. But compare it with many a question put by the sages of earth. Consider it side by side with the ponderings and the misgivings, the inquisitiveness and the apprehensions of a great Philosopher, when he interrogates the Builder of the Universe, and sets himself in array, face to face, with Jehovah.

Nay, I have heard a very intelligent person

of mature age betray a confusion of thought altogether as laughable as that of the poor boy. She had been to see a captious old lady whom her father, in his youth, had once intended to marry. "And how did you like her?" said I. "Not at all," she replied; "oh, you don't know how glad I am that father did not marry her; I never should have liked her, I am sure." As if, marry whom he might, she must have been born, *she* herself, with precisely the same preferences, prejudices and opinions!

"Oh, mother!" said little Mary, aged two years and a half at the time, looking up as she heard a noise, and blushing from head to foot, "*I hear a bad smell,* — 'taint me nor brother. It was an old man in the next house;" hemming loudly and suddenly, with a cough. Modesty is one thing, — squeamishness about children another; and this is really too good to be lost.

I remember a little boy who was a lexicographer from his birth, a language-master and a philosopher. From the hour he was able to ask for a piece of bread and butter, he never hesitated for a word, not he! If one wouldn't serve, another would, with a little twisting and turning. He assured me one day, when I was holding him by the hand rather tighter than he wished (he was but just able to speak at the time), that I should *choke* his hand; at another, he came to me all out of breath, to announce that a man was below *shaving* the wall. Upon due inquiry, it turned out that he was only *whitewashing*. But how should he know the difference between whitewash and lather, a big brush and a little one? Show me, if you can, a prettier example of synthesis or generalization, or a more beautiful adaptation of old words to new purposes. I have heard another complain of a school-fellow for *winking* at him *with his lip;* and he took the affront very much to heart, I assure you, and would not be pacified till the matter was cleared up.

Another, now at my elbow, hardly five, has just been prattling about the *handle* of a pin, meaning the *head;* to him *shavings* were *board-ravellings*, above a twelvemonth ago, and I never shall forget his earnestness about what he called the *necklace* of the gate, — a heavy iron chain with a large weight swinging to it, — which a wood-sawyer had forgotten to replace after finishing his work.

It is but yesterday that a little boy, being asked by an elder sister in my presence what a *widow* was — he had been talking about a widow — replied, *A poor woman that goes out a-washing.* What better definition would you have? At home or abroad, is not the poor widow always a-washing,—now the floors of a wealthier neighbor, and the clothes of somebody who happens not to be a widow,— and now with her own tears the face of her little baby, that lies half asleep and half sobbing in her lap? Other children talk about the *bones* in peaches,—osteologists are they; and others, when they have the toothache, aver that it *burns* them. Of such is the empire of poetry. I have heard another give a public challenge in these words to every child that came near, as she sat upon the doorstep with a pile of tamarind-stones, nut-shells, and pebbles lying before her: "Ah! I've got *many-er* than you!" That child was a better grammarian than Lindley Murray; and her wealth, in what was it unlike the hoarded and useless wealth of millions?

Not long ago, while passing through a narrow, unfrequented street, my attention was attracted by two little girls at play together: one a perfect tomboy, with large laughing eyes, and a prodigious quantity of hair; the other a little timid creature, altogether too shy to look up as I passed. The romp was balancing her body over the gate, and the little prude was looking at her. On the opposite side of the way were two smart-looking boys, whom I did not observe till I heard a sweet, clear voice at my elbow saying—almost singing, indeed—" I'll give oo a *kith* if oo want one!" I stopped and heard the offer repeated by the shy looking puss, while the romp stared at her with her mouth wide open, and the boys cleared out with a laugh, being too shame-faced to profit by the offer. Verily, verily, men *are* but children of a larger growth — *and women too.*

There was the language of truth, of innocence, of unadulterated nature! There are no mealy-mouthed human creatures among the pure. But lo! that child is going forth into the world, leaving behind her the green and beautiful places, haunted with wild flowers, where everything appeared in the language of truth; and after a little time, with far less purity, she may blush and tremble at every thought of being kissed, with or without her leave. And the poor boys,—anon they are to be the pursuers, and pray and beseech, where, but for a newly-acquired and counterfeit nature, they might loiter along by the wayside, and be sure of a call from the rosy lips and bright eyes that hovered about their path. Poor boys!

But children are wonderful for their courage, their patience, and their fortitude. I have known a little boy completely worn out by watching and suffering, tear off the bandages at last, and, looking up into the face of a woman who watched over him, say to her with a sweet smile,—"Georgee muss die, Chamber (her name was Chambers), *Georgee muss die — Georgee want to die.*" And he did die, with that very smile upon his mouth.

Not many years ago, another was caught in a mill: they stopped the machinery, and took the wheel to pieces; but it was an hour and a half before they could free her entirely. During this time she threw her arms about her father's neck, and kissing him, whispered: "*Am I dead, papa?*" She died within two hours after she was liberated. One might almost expect to see winglets of purple and gold, budding before death, from between the shoulders of such a child.

The *reasoning* of the little creatures, too, is always delightful; and if you are good-natured enough to follow them through their own little demonstrations, without insisting upon the language of a syllogism, always *conclusive.* Take two or three examples in proof: A child about three years of age, unperceived by its mother, followed her down cellar, and, when its mother returned, was left there. By-and-by the little thing was missed: inquiries were made in every quarter; the whole neighborhood was alarmed; the well searched, the hen-house, the barn, the very pigsty; but all in vain. At last, somebody had occasion to go into the cellar, and there, upon the bottom step of the stairs, the little creature was found, sitting by herself, as still as death, and purple with cold. Half frantic with joy, the mother snatched her up, and, running to the fire with her, asked her why she did not cry. "*I toudn't, ma,*" was the reply,—"I toudn't, ma, —*it war tho dark!*" After all, now, was not that a capital reason?—was it not the truth?

How many are there who cannot, or will not cry, even to their Father above, because *it is so dark.* Another child of about the same age used to lie awake and chatter by the hour, after she went to bed. Out of all patience with her one night, her bedfellow said to her, —

"Will you hold your tongue, Lucinda, and let me go to sleep?"

"No, I *tan't.*"

"You can't, — why not, pray?"

"Cause it *mates my tomach ache, Ant Rachel!*"

And even that child — why do you laugh at her? — didn't she tell the truth? and was not that a capital reason? How many grown people are there who *cannot hold their tongues*—and, if the truth were told, because *it makes their stomach ache!* or for some other reason not half so much to the purpose.

They are decided politicians, too. A friend of mine has a boy just able to speak.

"Houyah for Jackson!" said he one day, before his father.

"Why, Charles! why do you hurra for Jackson — I am not a Jackson man."

"Don't tare 'foo aint — I ar!" was the reply.

A *leader*, of course, for the next generation — of those who are to think for themselves.

Their childish cunning, too, is exquisite. I remember seeing a little boy about four years of age bite his eldest sister's finger in play so as to leave a mark, for which he was chidden by his mother, whereupon he stole away to his sister and put his finger into her mouth, and told her to *bite:* she refused, he insisted; after a good deal of persuasion, she yielded. "Harder! harder!" whispered he.

At last a mark appeared — a little *dent*. (You understand French, I hope.)

"*Now!*" said he, pulling her toward his mother. "*Now*" — his large eyes sparkling with triumph, and holding up his plump, rosy little finger, and making all sorts of faces — "*Now! tum to mother oosef!*"

Was there ever a better illustration of the Thistlewood Plot — of the Gunpowder Plot — or of that policy which, here as well as there, makes offences profitable to the informer? That boy was but another Vidocq; or another First Consul of the French Empire.

And have you never, when riding by in a stage-coach, seen a little fellow at the window or the door of a house in the country crying as if his very heart would break? Did not he always stop till you got by, — and then didn't he always begin again? with the same look, the same voice, and the same outcry, refusing to be comforted? These are the fellows for office — he only wanted an augmentation of salary; that was all — and I dare say he got it.

"Ah, ah, hourra! hourra! here's a fellow's birthday!" cried a boy in my hearing once. A number had got together to play ball; but one of them having found a birthday, and not only the birthday, but the very boy it belonged to, they all gathered about him, as if they had never witnessed a conjunction of the sort before. The very fellows for a committee of inquiry! — into the affairs of a national bank, too, if you please.

Never shall I forget another incident which occurred in my presence, between two other boys. One was trying to jump over a wheelbarrow — another was going by; he stopped, and, after considering a moment, spoke:

"I'll tell you what you can't do," said he.

"Well, what is it?"

"You can't jump down your own throat."

"Well, *you* can't."

"*Can't I though!*"

The simplicity of "Well, you can't," and the roguishness of "Can't I though!" tickled me prodigiously. They reminded me of sparring I had seen elsewhere — I should not like to say where — having a great respect for the Temples of Justice and the Halls of Legislation.

"I say *'tis* white-oak."

"I say it's red-oak."

"Well, I say it's white-oak."

"I tell ye 'taint white-oak."

Here they had joined issue for the first time.

"I say 'tis."

"I say 'taint."

"I'll bet ye ten thousand dollars of it."

"Well, I'll bet you ten thousand dollars!"

Such were the very words of a conversation I have just heard between two children, the elder about six, the other about five. Were not these miniature men? Stock-brokers and Theologians? or only *Land Speculators?*

"Well, my lad, you've been to meeting, hey?"

"Yes, sir."

"And who preached for you?"

"Mr. P——."

"Ah! and what did he say?"

"I can't remember sir, he put me out so."

"Put you out?"

"Yes, sir—he kept lookin' at my new clothes all meetin' time."

That child must have been a *close* observer. Will anybody tell me that he did not know what people go to meeting for?

It was but yesterday that I passed a fat

little girl with large hazel eyes, sitting by herself in a gateway, with her feet sticking straight out into the street. She was holding a book in one hand, and with a bit of stick in the other, was pointing to the letters.

"What's that?" cried she, in a sweet chirping voice; "*hey!* Look on! What's that, I say?—F—No—o—o—oh!" shaking her little head with the air of a school-mistress, who has made up her mind not to be trifled with.

It reminded me of another little girl somewhat older, who used to sit and play underneath my windows, and look down into the long green grass at her feet, and shake her head, and laugh and talk by the hour, as if she had a baby there, to the infinite amusement of all the neighborhood. That girl should have betaken herself to the stage. She was the very spirit of what may be called the familiar drama.

Talk as we may about children, their notions are sometimes both affecting and sublime; and their adventures more extraordinary than were the strangest of Captain Cook's, — more perilous than that of him who discovered America. I have known a child, not three years of age, and hardly tall enough to reach the round of a ladder, clamber up the side and along the roof, and seat himself on the ridge-pole of a two-story house, before they discovered him.

Very odd things occur to all parents, if they would but observe them, and treasure them — in the flowering of their children's hearts.

"When I am dead, sister Mary, I'll come back to see you, and you must save all the crumbs and feed me — won't ye, sister Mary?" said a little boy to his sister.

Upon full inquiry, I found that he had

associated the idea of little angels, that would fly about, with the pigeons belonging to a neighbor, which he had been accustomed to toll from the perch into the back-yard, with little crumbs of bread, saved at the table. On another occasion, he laid down his knife and fork, and looking up with the most perfect seriousness and apparent good faith, said, —

"Father, I mustn't eat any more fat meat."

"Why not, my boy?"

"God told me I must not."

"God! — when?"

"Last night, father."

Of course the child had been dreaming — so I urged the inquiry a little further:

"Did you see God?"

"Yes, father."

"And how did He look?"

"Oh, He looked like a — like a —" thoughtfully, and casting about for a comparison —

and then all at once he brightened up and said,—

"Like a woodchuck, father!"

For a moment I was thunder-struck — where could he have got such an idea? He had never seen a woodchuck in his life. Instead of laughing at the absurdity of the notion, however, I treated the matter very seriously, and after a while found that he had been on the watch at the window every day for nearly a month, to see a woodchuck which had escaped from a neighbor, and burrowed under our wood-house, and used to come out after nightfall to feed. The little fellow was perfectly honest — he had no idea of untruth or irreverence; others had seen the woodchuck, and he had not, and nothing occurred to him half so strange or mysterious for a comparison. It would not do to compare God with anything he had seen, and a woodchuck was the only thing he had not seen which corresponded at all with his notions of the Invisible.

But children have other characters. At times they are creatures to be afraid of. Every case I give, is a fact within my own observation. There are children, and I have had to do with them, whose very eyes were terrible: children who, after years of watchful and anxious discipline, were as indomitable as the young of the wild beast dropped in the wilderness; crafty, and treacherous, and cruel. And others I have known, who, if they live, *must* have dominion over the multitude; being evidently of them that, from the foundations of the world, have been always thundering at the gates of Power.

There sits a little girl with raisins in her lap. She had enough to spare a few minutes ago, but now she has given them all away, handful by handful, to a much older and more crafty child. She has not another left; and as she sits by him, and looks him up in the face, and asks him for one now and then *so* innocently, he keeps cramming them into his mouth, and occasionally doles one out to her with such a look! so strangely made up of reluctance and self-gratulation. And she, poor thing, whenever she gets one, affects to enjoy it prodigiously, shaking her head, and making a noise with her mouth as if it were crammed full. Just as the twig is bent, etc., etc.

And it is but the other day — only a week ago — I had an opportunity of seeing a similar case. A girl of eighteen months was overhauling her play-basket before a boy of seven. She was ready enough to show all her toys, but whatever he took into his hand, she would instantly reach after. Before two minutes were over, I found him playing the man of business, pretending to like what he did not, and to dislike what he most coveted. There were heaps of playthings strewed about over the floor. Among them were the remains of a little dog which had been sadly pulled to pieces, but which the boy took a decided fancy to, nevertheless. He kept his eye upon them, and after taking possession leaned over toward the little girl, and shook his head, and spoke in that peculiarly soothing voice, and with that coaxing manner, which are common to horse-dealers, and which children so well know how to counterfeit when they have a worthy object in view.

"Oh, the pretty teapot! Oh my! Mary want it," said he, turning it over and over, and carefully displaying the crooked nose, the warped handle, and the useless bottom, while he secured the dog.

That over, he tried his hand at a little Indian basket, talking all the time as fast as his tongue could run, in favor of the toys he had no relish for. A diplomatist in embryo, a chess-player, a merchant, a lawyer? What more can the best of them do? What more have they ever done?

I saw three children throwing sticks at a cow. She grew tired of her share in the game at last, and, holding down her head and shaking it, demanded a new deal. They cut and run. After getting to a place of comparative security, they stopped, and holding by the top of a board-fence, over which they had clambered, began to reconnoitre. Meanwhile another troop of children hove in sight, and, arming themselves with brickbats, began to approach the same cow; whereupon two of the others called out from the fence,—

"You Joe! you better mind! that's our cow!"

The plea was admitted without a demurrer, and the cow was left to be tormented by the legal owners. Hadn't these boys the law on their side?

A youth once lived with me who owned a little dog. One day I caught the dog worrying what I supposed to be a rat, and the boy standing over him and encouraging him. It proved to be a toad; the poor creature escaped during my interference. Before a month had gone over, the dog showed symptoms of hydrophobia, and I shot him. Not long after this I found the boy at a pump trying to keep a tub full, which appeared to have no bottom. I inquired what he was doing, and it turned out that he was trying to drown a *frog*. I asked the reason:

Because a *toad* had poisoned the poor little dog.

Here was a process of ratiocination worthy of any autocrat that ever breathed. Because A suffered soon after worrying B, therefore C shall be pumped to death. Precisely the case of Poland.

I know another little boy who once lost a favorite dog. About a week afterward the dog reappeared, and the boy was the happiest creature alive. But something happened a little out of the way, which caused further inquiry, when it turned out that the new dog was not the old one, though astonishingly like. The only difference I could perceive was a white spot under the neck. Well, what does our boy do? receive the stranger with thankfulness, and adopt him with joy, for his extraordinary resemblance to a lost favorite? No, indeed; but he gives him a terrible thumping, and turns him neck-and-heels out of doors on a cold, rainy night! As if the poor dog had been guilty of personating another! How perfectly of a piece with the behavior of grown people who have cheated themselves, and found it out. Woe to the innocent and the helpless who lie in their path! or sleep in their bosom, or inhabit among their household gods!

But children are not merely unjust, and cruel, and treacherous, even as men are. Like men, they are murderers, mischief-makers, devils, at times. I knew two boys, the older not more than four, who caught a hen, and, having pulled out her eyes with crooked pins, they let her go; after which, on seeing her stagger and tumble about, and perhaps afraid of discovery, they determined to cut off her head. One was to hold her, and the other to perform the operation; but for a long while they could not agree upon their respective shares in the performance. At last they hit upon a precious expedient. They laid her upon the steps, put a board over her body, upon which one of the two sat, while the other sawed off her head with a dull case-knife. Parents! Fathers! Mothers! What child of four years of age was ever capable of such an act, without a long course of preparation? for neglect is preparation. Both were murderers, and their parents were their teachers. If "the child is father of the man," what is to become of such children? If it be true that "just as the twig is bent the tree's inclined," how much have you to answer for? If "men are but children of a larger growth," watch your children forever, by day and by night! pray for them forever, by night and by day! and not as children, but as *Men* of a smaller growth, — as men with most of the evil passions, and with all the evil propensities, that go to make man terrible to his fellow-men, his countenance hateful, his approach a fiery pestilence, and his early death a blessing, even to his father and mother!

GOODY GRACIOUS!

AND THE

FORGET-ME-NOT.

ONCE there was a little bit of a thing,— not more than so high,— and her name was Ruth Page; but they called her Teenty-Tawnty, for she was the daintiest little creature you ever saw, with the smoothest hair and the brightest face; and then she was always playing about, and always happy: and so the people that lived in that part of the country, when they heard her laughing and singing all by herself at peep of day, like little birds after a shower, and saw her running about in the edge of the wood after tulips and butterflies, or tumbling head-over-heels in the long rich grass by the river side, with her little pet lamb or her two white pigeons always under her feet, or listening to the wild bees in the apple-blossoms, with her sweet mouth "all in a tremble," and her happy eyes brimful of sunshine, — they used to say that she was no child at all, or no child of earth, but a Fairy-gift, and that she must have been dropped into her mother's lap, like a handful of flowers, when she was half asleep; and so they wouldn't call her Ruth Page, — no indeed, that they wouldn't! — but they called her little Teenty-Tawnty, or the little Fairy; and they used to bring her Fairy Tales to read, till she couldn't bear to read anything else, and wanted to be a Fairy herself.

Well, and so one day, when she was out in the sweet-smelling woods, all alone by herself, singing, " Where are you going, my pretty maid, my pretty maid?" and watching the gold-jackets, and the blue dragon-flies, and the sweet pond-lilies, and the bright-eyed glossy eels, and the little crimson-spotted fish, as they "coiled and swam," and darted hither and thither, like "flashes of golden fire," and then huddled together, all of a sudden, just underneath the green turf where she sat, as if they saw something, and were half frightened to death, and were trying to hide in the shadow; well and so — as she sat there, with her little naked feet hanging over and almost touching the water, singing to herself, "My face is my fortune, sir, she said! sir, she said!" and looking down into a deep sunshiny spot, and holding the soft smooth hair away from her face with both hands, and trying to count the dear little fish before they got over their fright, all at once she began to think of the Water-Fairies, and how cool and pleasant it must be to live in these deep sunshiny hollows, with green turf all about you, the blossoming trees and the blue skies overhead, the bright gravel underneath your feet, like powdered stars, and thousands of beautiful fish for playfellows! all spotted with gold and crimson, or winged with rose-leaves, and striped with faint purple and burnished silver, like the shells and flowers of the deep sea, where the moonlight buds and blossoms forever and ever; and then she thought if she could only just reach over, and dip one of her little fat rosy feet into the smooth shining water, — just once — only once, — it would be *so* pleasant! and she should be *so* happy! and then, if she could but manage to scare the fishes a little — a very little — that would be such glorious fun, too, — wouldn't it, you?

Well and so — she kept stooping and stooping, and stretching and stretching, and singing to herself all the while, "Sir, she said! sir, she said! I'm going a-milking, sir, she said!" till just as she was ready to tumble in, head first, something jumped out of the bushes behind her, almost touching her as it passed, and went plump into the deepest part of the pool! saying, "*Once! once!*" with a booming sound, like the tolling of a great bell under water, and afar off.

"Goody gracious! what's that?" screamed little Ruth Page; and then, the very next moment, she began to laugh and jump and clap her hands, to see what a scampering there was among the poor silly fish, and all for nothing! said she; for out came a great good-natured bull-frog, with an eye like a bird, and a big bell-mouth, and a back all frosted over with precious stones, and dripping with sunshine; and there he sat looking at her awhile, as if he wanted to frighten her away; and then he opened his great lubberly mouth at her, and bellowed out, "*Once! once!*" and vanished.

"Luddy tuddy! who cares for you?" said little Ruth; and so, having got over her fright, she began to creep to the edge of the bank once more, and look down into the deep water, to see what had become of the little fish that were so plentiful there, and so happy but a few minutes before. But they were all gone, and the water was as still as death; and while she sat looking into it, and waiting for them to come back, and wondering why they should be so frightened at nothing but a bull-frog, which they must have seen a thousand times, the poor little simpletons! and thinking she should like to catch one of the smallest and carry it home to her little baby-brother, all at once a soft shadow fell upon the water, and the scented wind blew her smooth hair all into her eyes, and as she put up both hands in a hurry to pull it away, she heard something like a whisper close to her ear, saying, "*Twice! twice!*" and just then the trailing branch of a tree swept over the turf, and filled the whole air with a storm of blossoms, and she heard the same low whisper repeated close at her ear, saying, "*Twice! twice!*" and then she happened to look down into the water, — and what do you think she saw there?

"Goody gracious, mamma! is that you?" said poor little Ruth; and up she jumped, screaming louder than ever, and looking all about her, and calling "Mamma, mamma! I see you, mamma! you needn't hide, mamma!" But no mamma was to be found.

"Well, if that isn't the strangest thing!" said little Ruth, at last, after listening a few minutes, on looking all round everywhere, and up into the trees, and away off down the river-path, and then toward the house. "If I didn't think I saw my dear good mamma's face in the water, as plain as day, and if I didn't hear something whisper in my ear and say, '*Twice! twice!*'"—and then she stopped, and held her breath, and listened again—"If I didn't hear it as plain as I ever heard anything in my life, then my name isn't Ruth Page, that's all, nor Teenty-Tawnty neither!" And then she stopped, and began to feel very unhappy and sorrowful; for she remembered how her mother had cautioned her never to go near the river, nor into the woods alone, and how she had promised her mother many and many a time never to do so, never, never! And then the tears came into her eyes, and she began to wish herself away from the haunted spot, where she could kneel down and say her prayers; and then she looked up to the sky, and then down into the still water, and then she thought she would just go and take one more peep — only one — just to see if the dear little fishes had got over their fright, and then she would run home to her mother, and tell her how forgetful she had been, and how naughty, and ask her to give her something that would make her remember her promises. Poor thing! little did she know how deep the water was, nor how wonderfully she had escaped! once, once! twice, twice! and still she ventured a third time.

Well and so — don't you think, she crept along — crept along — to the very edge of the green, slippery turf, on her hands and knees, half trembling with fear, and half laughing to think of that droll-looking fat fellow, with the big bell-mouth, and the yellow breeches, and the grass-green military jacket, turned up with buff and embroidered with gems, and the bright golden eye that had so frightened her before, and wondering in her little heart if he would show himself again; and singing all the while, as she crept nearer and nearer, "Nobody asked you, sir, she said! sir, she said! nobody asked you, sir, she said!" till at last she had got near enough to look over, and see the little fishes there tumbling about by dozens, and playing bo-peep among the flowers that grew underneath the bank, and multiplied by thousands in the clear water, when, all at once, she felt the turf giving way, and she put out her arms and screamed for her mother. Goody gracious! how she did scream! and then something answered from the flowing waters underneath, and from the flowering trees overhead, with a mournful sweet sound, like wailing afar off, "*Thrice! thrice!*" and the flashing waters swelled up, saying, "*Thrice! thrice!*" and the flowering branch of the tree swept over the turf, and the sound was the same, "*Thrice! thrice!*" and in she went headlong, into the deepest part of the pool, screaming with terror, and calling on her mother to the last: poor mother!

Well and so — when she came to herself, where do you think she was? Why, she was lying out in the warm summer air, on a green bank, all tufted with cowslips and violets and clover-blossoms, with a plenty of strawberries underneath her feet, and the bluest water you ever saw all round her, murmuring like the rose-lipped sea-shells; and the air was full of singing-birds, and there was a little old woman looking at her, with the funniest cap, and a withered face not bigger than you may see when you look at the baby through the big end of a spy-glass: the cap was a morning-glory, and it was tied underneath the chin with bleached cobweb, and the streamers and bows were just like the colors you see in a soap-bubble.

"Goody gracious! where am I now?" said little Ruth.

"Yes, my dear, that's my name," said the little old woman, dropping a low courtesy, and then spinning round two or three times, and squatting down suddenly, so as to make what you call a cheese.

"Why, you don't mean to say that's your real name," whispered little Ruth.

"To be sure it is! just as much as — and pray, my little creature, what's your name?"

"Mine! oh my name is Ruth Page, *only* Ruth Page," and up she jumped, and spun round among the strawberries and flowers, and tried to make a courtesy like the little old woman, and then they both burst out a-laughing together.

"Well," said Goody Gracious, "you're a nice, good-natured, funny little thing, I'll say that for you, as ever I happened to meet with; but haven't you another and a prettier name, hey?"

"Why, sometimes they call me Little Teenty-Tawnty," said Ruth.

"Fiddle-de-dee, I don't like that name any better than the other: we must give you a new name," said the little old woman; "but first tell me"—and she grew very serious, and her little sharp eyes changed color—"first tell me how you happened to be here, in the very heart of Fairy-land, with nobody to take care of you, and not so much as a wasp or a bumble-bee to watch over you when you are asleep."

"Indeed, and indeed, ma'am, I don't know,"

said little Ruth; "all I do know is, that I have been very naughty, and that I am drowned, and that I shall never see my poor dear mamma any more!" And then she up and told the whole story to the little old woman, crying bitterly all the while.

"Don't take on so, my little dear, don't, don't!" said Goody Gracious; and out she whipped what appeared to Ruth nothing but a rumpled leaf of the tiger-lily, and wiped her eyes with it. "Be a good child, and, after a trial of three days in Fairy-land, if you want to go back to your mother you shall go, and you may carry with you a token to her that you have told the truth."

"Oh, bless your little dear old-fashioned face," cried Ruth; "oh, bless you, bless you! only give me a token that will make me always remember what I have promised my poor dear mother, and I shall be so happy, and I won't ask for anything else."

"What, neither for humming-birds, nor gold-fish, nor butterflies, nor diamonds, nor pearls, nor anything you have been wishing for so long, ever since you were able to read about Fairy-land?"

"No, ma'am; just give me a ring of wheat-straw, or a brooch from the ruby-beetle, if you like, and I shall be satisfied."

"Be it so; but, before I change you to a fairy, you must make choice of what you want to see in Fairy-land for three days running; for, at the end of that time, I shall change you back again, so that if you are of the same mind then, you may go back to your mother, and, if not, you will stay with us forever and ever."

"Forever and ever?" said Ruth, and she trembled; "please ma'am, I should like to go now, if it's all the same to you."

"No! but take this flower;" and, as she

spoke, she stooped down, and pulled up a forget-me-not by the roots, and breathed upon it, and it blossomed all over. "Take this root," said she, "and plant it somewhere, and tend it well, and at any time after three days, if you get tired of being here, all you have to do will be just to pull it up out of the earth, and wish yourself at home, and you will find yourself there in a moment, in your own little bed."

"Goody gracious! you don't say so!"

"But I do say so."

"I declare, I've a good mind to try!"

"What, pull it up before you have planted it? No, no, my dear. It must be left out threescore and twelve hours, and be watered with the dews and the starlight of the South Sea, where you are now, thousands and thousands of miles from your own dear country; but there is one thing I would have you know before you plant the flower."

"If you please, ma'am," said little Ruth.

"It is given to you, my dear, to help you correct your faults; you mean to do right, and you try pretty hard, but you are *so* forgetful, you say."

"Yes, ma'am."

"Well, now, but remember — just so long as you tend this plant with care, and water it every day at the same hour, — every day, mind you, and at the same hour, — you will be growing better."

Ruth was overjoyed.

"But," continued the fairy, "if you neglect it for a single day, it will begin to droop and wither, the leaves will change, and some of the blossoms will drop off, and your mother will begin to feel unhappy and low-spirited."

"Oh, yes; but I never shall, ma'am — never, *never!*"

"Don't be too sure; and if you neglect it

for two whole days running, all the flowers will drop off but one, and your mother will take to her bed, and nobody but you will know what ails her."

Poor Ruth began to tremble, and the tears came in her eyes.

"But," continued the fairy, "*but* if you should neglect it for three days running, my poor child — but for three days running — the last flower will drop off, and your mother will die of a broken heart."

"Oh, mercy, mercy!" cried poor little Ruth. "Oh, take it! take it! I wouldn't have it for the world!" and she flung it down upon the loose earth, and shook her little fingers, just as if something had stung her.

"It is too late now. See, my dear, it has already taken root, and now there is no help for it. Remember! your mother's health, happiness and life depend upon that flower.

Watch it well! And now, daughter of earth," and, as she spoke, she stooped, and pulled up a whole handful of violets, dripping with summer rain, and repeating the words, "Daughter of earth, away! Rosebud, appear!" shook the moisture all over her; and instantly the dear child found herself afloat in the air, with pinions of purple gauze, bedropped with gold, with millions of little fairies all about her, swarming like butterflies and blossoms after a pleasant rain, and welcoming their sister Rosebud to Fairyland.

"Well," thought Rosebud, — we must call her Rosebud now, — "well, if this being a little fairy isn't one of the pleasantest things!" and then she recollected that she had only three days to stay there and see the sights, and she looked round her to ask if there was anybody near to help her, and take charge of her, and tell her what to do, and where to go.

"Daughter," said a sweet voice that she knew, though it appeared to come out, and steal up from the leaves of another morning-glory, — "Daughter!"

"Mother," said Rosebud.

"You may have your choice to-day of these three things, — a butterfly-hunt, a wedding, or a play."

"Oh, a wedding, a wedding!" said Rosebud. "Oh, I have always wanted to see a wedding!"

"Be it so," said the voice; and instantly a sweet wind arose, and lifted her up, and swept her, and thousands more like her, over the blue deep, so swiftly that nothing could be seen but a mist of sparkles here and there, till they all found themselves on the seashore, at the mouth of a deep sparry cave, all hung about with the richest moss, and lighted with pearls in clusters, and with little patches of glowworms, and carpeted with the wings of butterflies. In the midst were a multitude of little fairies, hovering and floating over a throne of spider-net ivory, on which lay the bride, with a veil of starlight, interwoven with the breath of roses, covering her from head to foot, and falling over the couch, like sunshine playing on clear water.

By and by a faint, strange murmuring was heard afar off, like the ringing of lily-bells to the touch of the honey-bees, growing louder and louder, and coming nearer and nearer every moment. Rosebud turned toward the sea with all the other fairies, and held her breath; and after a few moments, a fleet of little ships, with the most delicate purple and azure sails, so thin that you could see the sky through them, came tilting along over the sea, as if they were alive, — and so they were, — and drew up, as if in order of battle, just before the mouth of the cave; and then a silver trumpet sounded on the shore, and a swarm of hornets appeared, whizzing and whirring all about the cave; and then there was another trumpet, and another, about as loud as you may hear from a caged blue-bottle, and compliments were interchanged, and a salute fired, which frightened the little lady-fairies into all sorts of shapes, and made the little fairy-bride jump up and ask if her time had come, though, to tell you the truth, the noise did not appear much more terrible to Rosebud than her little brother's pop-gun; and then, a sort of barge, not unlike the blossom of a sweet pea in shape, was manned from the largest of the fleet, and, when it touched the bright sparkling sand, out leaped a little prince of a fellow, with a bunch of white feathers in his hat, plucked from the moth-miller, a sword like the finest cambric needle belted about his waist, and the most unimpeachable smallclothes.

This turned out to be the bridegroom; and after a few more flourishes, and not a little pulling and hauling among the bridesmaids, the bride and the bridegroom stood up together, and looked silly and sheepish, as if butter wouldn't melt in their mouths; and after listening awhile to an old droning-beetle, without hearing a word he said, they bowed and courtesied, and made some sort of a reply, nobody could guess what; and then forth stepped the master of ceremonies, a priggish-looking grasshopper, with straw-colored tights, and a fashionable coat, single-breasted, and so quakerish, it set poor little

Rosebud a-laughing, in spite of all she could do, every time she looked at his legs; and *then!* out flew the ten thousand trumpeting bumble-bees, and the katydid grew noisier than ever, and the cricket chirruped for joy, and the bridegroom touched the bride's cheek, and pointed slyly toward a little heap of newly-gathered roses and violets, piled up afar off, in a shadowy part of the cave, just underneath a trailing canopy of changeable moss; the bride blushed, and the fairies tittered, and little Rosebud turned away, and wished herself at home, and instantly the bride and the bridegroom vanished! and the ships and the fairies! and the lights and the music! and Rosebud found herself standing face to face with the little withered old woman, who was looking mournfully at the drooping forget-me-not. The tears came into her eyes; and for the first time since the flower took root

— for the very first time — she began to think of her mother, and of her promise to the fairy; and she stooped down, in an agony of terror, and shame, and self-reproach, to see how it fared with her forget-me-not. Alas! it had already begun to droop and wither; and the leaves were changing color, and the blossoms were dropping off, and she knew that her mother was beginning to suffer.

"Oh that I had never seen the hateful flower!" cried Rosebud; and then instantly recollecting herself, she dropped upon her knees, and kissed it, and wept upon it, and the flower seemed refreshed by her tears; and when she stood up and looked into the face of the good little fairy, and saw her lips tremble, and the color change in her sweet mournful eyes, she felt as if she never should be happy again.

"Daughter of earth! child of the air!" said the fairy, "two more days remain to thee. What wouldst thou have?"

"Oh nothing! nothing! Let me but go back to my dear, dear mother, and I shall be so happy!"

"That cannot be. These trials are to prepare thee for thy return to her. Be patient, and take thy choice of these three things, — a tournament, a coronation, or a ball!"

"Goody gracious! how I *should* like to see a coronation!" cried Rosebud; and then she recollected herself, and blushed and courtesied, and said, "If you please, ma'am."

"Call me mother, my dear; in Fairy-land I am your mother."

"Well, mother," said Rosebud, the tears starting into her eyes and her heart swelling, as she determined never to call her mamma, no, never! "Well, mother, if you please, I would rather stay here and watch the flower; I don't want to see anything more in Fairyland; I've had enough of such things to last me as long as I live. But oh, if I should happen to fall asleep!"

"If you should, my dear, you will wake in season; but take your choice."

"Thank you, mother, but I choose to stay here."

At these words the fairy vanished, and Rosebud was left alone, looking at the dear little flower, which seemed to grow fresher and fresher, and more and more beautiful every minute, and wondering whether it would be so with her dear mamma; and then she fell a-thinking about her home, and how much trouble she had given her mother, and how much better she would always be, after she had got back to her once more; and then she fell asleep, and slept so soundly that she did not wake till the sun was up, and it was time to water the flower.

At first she was terribly frightened; but when she remembered what the fairy told her, she began to feel comfortable, and, lest something might happen, she took a little sea-shell that lay there, and running down to the water, dipped it up full, and was on her way back, thinking how happy her poor dear mamma would feel if she could only know *what* it was and *who* it was that made her so much better, when she heard the strangest and sweetest noises all about her in the air, as if the whole sky were full of the happiest and merriest creatures! and when she looked up, lo! there was a broad glitter to be seen, as if the whole population of Fairy-land were passing right over her head, making a sort of path like that you see at sunrise along the blue deep, when the waters are motionless, and smooth, and clear.

"Well," said she, looking up, "I *do* wonder where they are going so fast" — and then she stopped — "and I do think they might be civil enough just to let a body know; I dare say 'tis the coronation, or the butterfly hunt, or the tournament, or the — oh, how I should like to be there!"

No sooner was the wish uttered, than she found herself seated in a high gallery, as delicately carved as the ivory fans of the East; with diamonds and ostrich-feathers all about and below her, and a prodigious crowd assembled in the open air, — with the lists open — a trumpet sounding — and scores of knights armed cap-a-pie, and mounted on dragon-flies, waiting for the charge. All eyes were upon her, and everybody about was whispering her name, and she never felt half so happy in her life; and she was just beginning to compare the delicate embroidery of her wings with that of her next neighbor, a sweet little Fairy, who sat looking through her fingers at a youthful champion below, and pouting, and pouting, as if she wanted everybody to know that he had jilted her, when she happened to see a little forget-me-not embroidered on his beaver; and she instantly recollected her promise, and cried out, "Oh, mamma! mamma!" and wished herself back again, where she might sit by the flower and watch over it, and never leave it, never! till her three days of trial were ended.

In a moment, before she could speak a word, or even make a bow to the nice little boy-fairy, who had just handed her up her glove on the point of a lance like a sunbeam, she found herself seated by the flower.

Poor little thing! It was too late! Every blossom had fallen off but one, and that looked unhealthy, and trembled when she breathed upon it. She thought of her mamma, and fancied she could see them carrying her up to bed, and all the doctors there, and nobody able to tell what ailed her; and she threw herself all along upon the grass, and wished all the fairies at the bottom of the Red Sea, and herself with them! And when she looked up, what do you think she saw? and where do you think she was? why, she was at the bottom of the Red Sea, and all the wonders of the Red Sea were about her, — chariots and chariot-wheels and the skeletons of war-horses, and mounted warriors, with heaps of glittering armor, and jewels of silver, and jewels of gold, and banner, and shield, and spear, with millions and millions of little sea-fairies, and

Robin Goodfellows, and giants and dwarfs, and the funniest looking monsters you ever did see; and the waters were all bright with fairy-lamps that were alive, and with ribbons that were alive, and with changeable flowers that swam about and whispered to each other in a language of their own; and there were great heaps of pearl washed up into drifts and ridges, and a pile of the strangest-looking old-fashioned furniture, of gold and ivory, and little mermaids with their dolls not longer than your finger, with live fishes for tails, jumping about and playing hide-and-seek with the sun-spots and star-fishes, and the striped water-snakes of the Indian seas — the most brilliant and beautiful of all the creatures that live there.

And while she was looking about her, and wondering at all she saw, she happened to think once more of the *forget-me-not*, and to wish herself back again! At that instant she heard a great heavy bell booming and tolling — she knew it was tolling — and she knew she was too late — and she knew that her mother was dead of a broken heart, — and she fell upon her face, and stretched forth her hands with a shriek, and prayed God to forgive her! and allow her to see her mother once more — only once more!

"Why, what ails the child?" whispered somebody that seemed to be stooping over her.

It was her mother's voice! and poor Ruth was afraid to look up, lest it should all vanish forever.

"Upon my word, Sarah," said another voice, — it was her father's; "upon my word, Sarah, I do not know; but the poor little creature's thoughts appear to have undergone another change. I have heard nothing to-day of the forget-me-not which troubled her so the first week, have you?"

"She has mentioned it but once to-day, and then she shuddered; but perhaps we had better keep it in the glass till we see whether it will bear to be transplanted, for she seems to have set her little heart upon having that flower live; I wish I knew why!"

"Do you, indeed, mamma?" whispered poor Ruth, still without looking up; "well, then, I will tell you. That flower was given me by a fairy to make me remember my promises to you, my poor, dear, dead mamma; and so long as I water that, every day at the same hour, so long I shall be growing better and better, and my poor dear mamma — boo-hoo! boo-hoo!" and the little thing began to cry as if she would break her heart.

"Why, this is stranger than all," said the father. "I can't help thinking the poor child would be rational enough now, if she hadn't read so many Fairy-books; but what a mercy it was, my dear Sarah, and how shall we ever be thankful enough, that you happened to be down there when she fell into the water."

"Ah!" Ruth Page began to hold her breath, and listen with the strangest feeling.

"Yes, Robert; but I declare to you I am frightened whenever I think of the risk I ran by letting her fall in, head first, as I did."

Poor Ruth began lifting her head by little and little, and to feel about, and pinch herself, to see if she was really awake, or only dreaming.

"And then, too, just think of this terrible fever, and the strange, wild poetry she has been talking, day after day, about Fairyland."

"Poetry! Fudge, Robert, fudge!"

Ruth looked up, full of amazement and joy, and whispered, "Fudge, father, fudge!" and the very next words that fell from her trembling lips as she sat looking at her mother, and pointing at a little bunch of forget-me-nots in full flower, that her mother had kept for her in a glass by the window, were these: "Oh, mother! dearest mother! what a terrible dream I have had!"

"Hush, my love, hush! and go to sleep, and we will talk this matter over when you are able to bear it."

"Goody gracious, mamma!"

"There she goes again!" cried the father; "now we shall have another fit!"

"Hush, hush, my love! you must go to sleep, now, and not talk any more."

"Well, kiss me, mamma, and let me have your hand to go to sleep with, and I'll try."

Her mother kissed the dear little thing,

and took her hand in hers, and laid her cheek upon the pillow, and, in less than five minutes, she was sound asleep, and breathing as she hadn't breathed before, since she had been fished out of the water, nearly three weeks back, on her way to Fairy-land.

CONTENTS

OF

PICKINGS AND STEALINGS.

Children's notions of theology, 1, 2, 13, 14, 22, 48, 70, 72, 132, 134, 166, 168, 178, 265, 283.
Children's notions of the Bible, 2, 39, 41, 148, 149, 163, 174, 228.
Children's notions of heaven, 4, 19, 88, 101, 119, 145, 215, 224, 230, 238, 239, 265, 284.
Lessons for teachers, 2, 4, 5, 31, 43, 47, 66.
Children's notions of praying, 6, 11, 37, 42, 98, 118, 155, 161, 163, 166, 187, 254, 288.
Their notions of language, 7, 10, 15, 21, 120, 121, 153, 194, 251.
Their honesty, 2, 8, 12, 17, 78, 115, 119, 122, 125, 137, 195, 143, 257, 271, 274.
Their ideas of another world, 25, 30, 38, 127, 144, 193, 242, 270.
Their instincts, 16, 18, 27, 28, 31, 44, 69, 76, 80, 90, 108, 118, 141, 144, 167, 181, 263.
Their philosophy, 21, 163, 165, 183, 203.
Their politics, 23, 214, 254.
Their Sunday-school exercises, 22, 26, 31, 43, 47, 66, 142, 156, 164, 165, 187, 195, 205, 241, 266, 277, 280, 282.
Their imitation, 28, 85, 105, 146, 176, 181, 192, 204, 212, 219, 222, 232, 240.
Their selfishness, 29, 40, 79, 87, 116, 150, 151, 243, 267.
Their quibbles, 33, 67, 80, 231, 245, 286.
Their misapprehension of words, 2, 35, 112, 120, 121, 160, 223, 252, 264, 276, 282.

Their puzzling questions, 24, 72, 160, 178, 253, 268.
Their cunning, 33, 45, 46, 51, 73, 79, 82, 92, 106, 224, 228, 130, 134, 139, 158, 163, 169, 172, 202, 206, 259, 260, 273, 279, 286.
Their unselfishness, 49, 50.
Their foresight, 52, 90, 102, 188, 208.
Their self-complacency, 54, 71, 77.
Their metaphysics, 1, 72, 74, 96, 162, 170, 261.
Their explanations, 84, 95, 123, 130, 156, 183, 196, 246, 262, 282.
Their adroitness, 85, 89, 99, 103, 105, 122, 124, 125, 147, 152.
Their speculations, 90, 100, 109, 140, 180, 210, 275.
Their business qualities, 91.
Their naturalness, 93, 110, 114, 180, 181, 189, 201, 218, 220, 263, 272, 274, 291.
Their faith, 98, 177, 287.
Their influence, 115, 285
Their misapplication of words, 1, 48, 148, 162, 225.
Retribution, 128.
Example, 129, 267, 268.
A great mystery, 133, 217.
An etymologist, 136.
Their literalness, 134, 229, 235, 256, 268, 269, 277, 278, 279.
Their definitions, 156, 184, 257, 261, 262.
Their protestantism, 189, 190.
Their smartness, 197. *See* Cunning, 201, 240, 250, 264, 269, 289.
Their constructiveness, 198.
Yankee notions, 1, 199.
Their pluckiness, 216, 237, 247, 255.
Total depravity, 227.
Where mother is, 230, 287.
Their poetry, 230, 234, 270.
Liberty of Speech, 259, 260.

PICKINGS AND STEALINGS.

TROUBLESOME comforts are they at best, these Little Plagues; and yet, how on earth should we get along without them? Mysterious and wonderful in their perturbations and irregularities, they are continually amazing the wisest by their questionings, and startling whole neighborhoods with their strange outbreaks of inner life, as you may see by what follows. For a long while — many years, indeed — I have been in the habit of minuting down the stories that have come in my way about the little folks — the seedling cherubim — out of which, as the stars are smelted, the angels of God, who see His face forever, are to be recast and refashioned for the skies. Grains of gold are they, often gathered from street sweepings and rubbish; diamond-sparks which the great multitude, in their headlong hurry, overlook, but infinitely precious to the Philanthropist and the Philosopher. For example : —

No. 1. And this I had from the late John Pierpont, who related it of a grandchild, yet living, I hope.

"Aunt May-ee," said the little thing to her aunt, who was combing her hair, "I don't like Dod."

"Don't like God, Sissy! when He's so good to you, and gives you Aunt Mary and grandpa, and grandma, and ever so many friends to take care of you, — *why*, Sissy?"

"Well, but" — growing thoughtful and trying to escape — "well, but Sissy don't like black Dod."

"There isn't any black God, Sissy."

"*Then who made Chloe?*"

Did not that child reason?

No. 2. "'Top, mother!" said a little boy to his mother, who was reading to him about Abraham and Isaac, and had just come to the uplifted knife; "'top, mother! I don't want to hea any more. *I despise him.*" Did not that child *feel?* and is it conceivable that he meant what he said? Feeling his gorge rise, with abhorrence, it may be, and not understanding the awful significance of the threatened sacrifice, a type of what afterwards happened on Mount Moriah, where the Temple stands, he took that word which, in his little childish experience, best corresponded with his thought of horror and amazement that a father should put his child to death.

No. 3. And this reminds me of a little

girl, who had never learned to read, but used to take her Bible and sit down by herself in the corner, as all children do at times, and make believe read. One day, when the mother was very busy, the child wanted to hear about Noah and the Ark. The mother had read over certain passages aloud so often, that the child had got them by heart. She opened at the place, and gave her little one the book in her lap. After awhile, the child began to murmur to herself — the mother listened — and the little thing read as follows, with the greatest possible seriousness and unction: "And the Lord said, unto Noah, Come out, thou and thy wife, and thy sons' wives and thy daughters, and — *balancez!*"

The dear little puss had just begun to go to the dancing-school. What wonder that she didn't always know her head from her heels?

No. 4. Another little girl, who had been favored with glimpses of the upper sky, having been told by her mother that she was *always* surrounded by guardian angels, grew very thoughtful, and, after drawing a long breath, looked up and said, "Mamma, do you mean *really* that *all the whole time* they are with me?" On receiving a solemn assurance in the affirmative, she exclaimed with an impatient fling, "Well, really, I *should* like to be alone a little while, *sometimes*."

What a lesson for the mother! If children are allowed to dabble with mysteries like these, without explanation, they cannot be otherwise than shocking sometimes, like a Leyden jar; and if they are, whose fault is it? Either more or less ought to have been told that dear little, honest baby.

No. 5. But children have wonderful foresight, and often reach conclusions by a sort of intuitive logic, as women do — flashing the truth upon us without preparation, and forecasting the future, as if suddenly gifted with second sight. A little boy, having been told by his parents that he couldn't go to church because he was too small, answered with a toss of the head, "Well, you'd better take me now, for when I get bigger, I may not want to go!" To which I say, Bravo! my little man! Such a reply ought to throw the doors of any church wide open to you, as to a glorified spirit — in embryo.

No. 6. A little girl knelt down by her mother's knee to say her prayers, before going to bed. After finishing the Lord's Prayer, she went on to offer up her little petitions for every separate member of the family, and at last came to the youngest, who, having been rather naughty that day, was out of favor: "And please God make Lucy a good little girl, and make —" here she was suddenly interrupted by Lucy, who burst out with — "Here you! stop that! I'll do my own praying myself, I thank you!"

Who would not sympathize with such a child, under such circumstances, even though both were at an infant prayer-meeting? And who is there who would not shrink from being prayed for to his face anywhere, after such a fashion?

No. 7. Their notions of language, too, are sometimes of the drollest, as where the poor boy used that unfortunate word *despise*, when he meant only to express horror and astonishment. "How did you fall — *backward?*" said a mother to a child who was just coming to herself and gasping for breath, after a heavy fall. "*Backward*, mamma! no indeed — I fell *accidentally.*"

No. 8. A dear little boy, anything but pious, though happy and cheerful, and about as good as most boys of his age, had been listening patiently for a long while to his mother's account of heaven — likening it to a great everlasting Sabbath-school. At last he looked up, with a troubled countenance, and said in a whisper, "But mamma, don't you think God would let me have a little devil come up and play with me sometimes, when I have been very good?"

No. 9. Another little fellow, on his way home from his church with his mother, seemed astonished at the crowds he saw. After walking awhile without speaking, he came out with, "Why mamma, I should think God would be tired making so many people." Here was an embryo theologian for you! And yet he had probably never heard of the Scripture, where it is said that God *re-*

pented of His making man. Nor was he quite prepared to understand why such crowds were ever made, nor what they were good for, seeing how they behaved, and how they were employed, and how they dressed, and how they chattered. If Babels were scattered of yore, why not now — if they try to scale the heavens by a forbidden path, or to carry their bulwarks by assault, as most of the nations do?

No. 10. A little girl who had learned her letters and all her lessons by the help of a pictured primer, but had never learned to put them together, opened her book one day at the picture of a *quail*, with its name underneath, in large letters. After studying a long while, she seemed to catch the idea, and called it a *pigeon* — a word she could not pronounce, though she knew the bird well enough, and out she came with "Q. U. A. I. L.

—*fidget*"— with such an air of triumph and self-complacency, it was never forgotten.

No. 11. Children's prayers — if they are indeed prayers — must be acceptable on earth as well as in heaven; and he must indeed be heartless, or worse, who would think slightingly of them, although, sooth to say, they are sometimes hard to bear. For example: a little girl, on having her hair smartly pulled by her little brother, while saying her prayers, went on for awhile, without turning her head, in the same low monotone, "and please God, excuse me for a minute, while I kick Neddy." Tell me that child was without understanding what is meant by prayer! or that she meant to abuse the privilege. No such thing — though, to be sure, she may have misunderstood some of its functions. Had she not been a believer, she would have kicked Neddy at once, without asking leave — would she not?

No. 12. But children must not be allowed to counterfeit or pretend. Encourage them to be honest, even in prayer — honest even at church. A fine, hearty little fellow, who had been treated with his first circus on Saturday, and to his first church-service the next Sabbath-morning, sat quietly enough, as everybody acknowledged, for the first half hour: and then he began to grow uneasy, and fidget in his seat, until he was admonished by his mother more than once. Worn to death at last, he groaned out loud enough to be heard in the neighboring pews, "O dear! I'd rather go to two circuses than one meeting!" Of course he told the truth; and of course he ought to have been patted on the back, and encouraged for his downright honesty.

No. 13. Quart pots don't hold a gallon — though pint bottles are sometimes said to hold a quart in certain establishments; and we must be wary of packing and crowding these earthen vessels, before they are hooped and strengthened. A small boy, not otherwise remarkable, though mischievous, adroit and playful, had been talked to, till he was out of all patience with a clergyman, about the omnipresence of God. It was pretty clear, from what followed, that he had begun to be somewhat sceptical, and he determined to lay a trap for his teacher. One day, when they were riding together, the following conversation was had : —

"Didn't you tell me, sir," said our young master, "that God is everywhere?"

"Yes, my child."

"Is he in this carriage?"

"Yes."

"Is he in my hat?"

"Yes — yes."

"Is he in my pocket?"

"Yes, child"—rather impatiently.

"Hurrah! now I've got you! I ain't got no pocket!" was the clincher.

What a lesson for that clergyman! If, as Goethe says, Hamlet was an oak planted in a china vase, intended for a rose-tree, so that when the plant grew, the pot was shattered, what was likely to happen to that child, if the omnipresence of God had been suffered to take root in his young, unprepared heart?

No. 14. Another child, afflicted with similar misgivings, took a different course to satisfy his inward longings. After propounding every conceivable question at the breakfast-table one day, he clenched the whole with, "Is God in this sugar-bowl?" "Certainly," said his mother. Whereupon, with a whoop, he clapped his hand on the bowl, and shouted, "Ah, ha! now I've got you, old fellow!"

So much for misunderstanding the most obvious truth, namely, that, although men are but children of a larger growth, children are not often philosophers, theologians, or giants—Mozart to the contrary notwithstanding; and that, in training them for another world, they are to be uplifted, not overborne, with mystery.

No. 15. Another little chap of three years only, met his father on his return from a long journey, exclaiming, "O papa, I've got a tory of *interet* to tell you. Dis mornin' mamma was writin' in the parlor, an' a gate, big, yeller fly comed in at the open window, an' it kep sayin' *sizzum, sizzum, sizzum,* three times, an' it *beed* my hand with its foot, and its foot was hot!"

Had not this child pretty decided notions of what is meant by the song of a "bumble bee," and the sting? Let him alone for that.

No. 16. The same boy, having thrown something valuable into the fire, was taken to task by his father, who, after remonstrating with him awhile on the enormity of his transgression, wound up with, "Why, my dear child, if you go on in this way, just think what a dreadful boy you will be, when you grow up!" At this, the little fellow's face brightened all over, and he exclaimed, "Why papa! I shall be yest like ee yobber kitten, sant I?"—alluding to the autobiography of a very disreputable fast kitten, who, or rather *which*, had taken to the highway at an early age, and is therefore a special favorite with children of all ages—like most of Mayne Reid's heroes, or Jonathan Wild, or Jack Sheppard.

No. 17. And this reminds me of a similar case, where well-meant instruction was painfully misunderstood by a promising little fellow, who was very fond of Bible-stories with illustrations. His mother was showing him a picture of Daniel in the lion's den, with the old lions ramping and tearing their prey to tatters, and a young lion — a cub — looking on. Just when she had begun to congratulate herself on the success of her teaching, the child cried out, "O mamma! look! look! the little one won't get any!"

N. B.— Beware of cramming and overloading. Beware also of expecting too much in this world. But, above, all, beware of misunderstanding yourself in your children!

No. 18. Yet more. A little girl having been brought up on the song "I want to be an angel!" had evidently been pondering the manners, habits, occupations and usages of that fraternity, until at length she came out decidedly with, "No mamma — I don't want to be an angel!"

"Not want to be an angel! Why, Susie!" exclaimed the mother, greatly shocked at the child's hopeless condition; "and why not, pray?"

"'Cause, mamma, I don't want to lose all my pretty close, an' wear fedders, like a hen!"

There's truthfulness for you — worth its weight in gold — a string of "Orient pearls at random strung."

No. 19. Another little fairy, having been carefully trained to a proper estimate of the becoming in attire, was taken into a room to see her dead grandmother in her coffin. She looked very grave at first, and then sorrowful, and after a minute or two said, in a low, sweet, trembling voice, with her little hand stealing slowly into her mother's hand, "Has grandmamma gone to heaven in that ugly cap, mamma?"

No. 20. Little mischiefs, at the best, I have said — are they not? Just read the following, and say no, if you dare! A youngster in Peoria, Illinois, while ransacking his sister's portfolio, came across a package of love-letters carefully tied up with a blue ribbon, and stowed snugly away; being her correspondence with a charming fellow, not, perhaps, to the liking of papa and mamma. These he took to the corner of a crowded thoroughfare, and, as he had seen the postman do, distributed them to the passers-by. His poor sister heard of the achievement after they were in general circulation; and *then!* —ask our friend Carlyle, after shooting Niagara; or Wendell Phillips — after Grant. See No. 53.

No. 21. I have just met with this: "A little lady of thirty months only, insists on calling a cane with a crooked handle, 'An umbrella without any clothes on.'" There's a philologist for you! And one, too, capable of giving a reason for what she says.

No. 22. A little boy in Scotland was asked by his Sabbath-school teacher what was meant by *regeneration*. "Being born again," he replied. "And would you not like to be born again, my little man?" said the teacher. "*No!*" answered the boy, with decided emphasis, greatly to the surprise of the good dominie. "And why not?" continued the latter. "For fear I might be born a lassie," said the boy. Was there ever a better reason, with the poor boy's understanding of the great mystery? So much for dabbling with metaphysics before the unprepared.

No. 23. And sometimes they have to do with politics and other worldly matters, — the social evil, perhaps, or woman's-rights, or universal suffrage. And why not? being what they are, miniature men and women, with the rights of both.

"Be you a Democat or a Republican?" said one of these President-makers in embryo, to another little fellow in a frilled apron. "No, I'm not either," was the indignant reply; "I belong to the Congregational Church." Of course he did; having been baptized into that denomination, when just old enough to be deeply impressed with the ceremony.

No. 24. A little girl of six years at the most, after her nurse had enlarged upon the character and attributes of the Old Evil One, till her blood ran cold, broke out with, "Auntie, if the devil is so wicked, why don't God kill him?" A question, by the way, which has "puzzled philosophers of all sects and ages," like the "cosmogony of the world," according to Oliver Goldsmith, and his delightful friend, Ephraim Jenkinson.

No. 25. Little Maud, five years old, was sitting on the floor, and trying to stitch like her mother. Suddenly looking up, after a long silence, she said, like one familiar with the gossip of the tea-table and the quilting-frame, "Mamma, I was thinking God must be getting quite along in years!" Of course, the poor little thing had never been so far indoctrinated, as to understand that, with God, a thousand years are as one day, or a watch in the night, and one day as a thousand years, with no past, and no future, but one everlasting present.

No. 26. Another little woman, being asked by her Sunday-school teacher, "What did the Israelites do after passing through the Red Sea?" answered, "I don't know, ma'am, but I guess they dried themselves." And why not, pray? What would be more likely?

No. 27. And here we have one exceedingly jealous for the Lord. A little boy, who, whenever he went out to play, was plagued and pestered by a little girl somewhat older — who squinted awfully, and was, it must be acknowledged, absolutely frightful — on being asked why he was always so *ugly* to Susie Bates, since God made Susie Bates as well as him, exclaimed, "O, Nurse Thompson, ain't you ashamed to talk in that way about the good Lord?"

Will you tell me that child did not reason? or that, *as* a child, he was irreverent, because he would not charge God foolishly, nor hold the Great Workman answerable for such workmanship?

No. 28. And this brings to mind the following incident: Some years ago my own little boy went, with his brother Robert, on a trip to the Islands. After awhile, he was caught making the most horrible faces at another little boy, somewhat older, who sat in the stern of the boat a long way off, but fronting them. Brother Robert interfered, and asked what possessed my little fellow—a good-natured, pleasant boy, as ever lived. "Why, don't you see? He's making faces at me all the time," said Pepper-pot. Upon further inquiry, it turned out that the strange boy was epileptic, or troubled with St. Vitus' dance, and all the faces he had been making were involuntary. Of course, it never entered the head of our little one that the faces he saw were God's work, or he would have lowered his voice to a whisper, as he always did in the Sabbath-school, when he asked about God.

No. 29. That children are curious, and inquisitive, and rather troublesome at times, we all know. But, if it were otherwise, how would they ever learn their a b *abs* in this world? In a Western village, a charming little widow had been made love to by a physician. "The wedding-day appointed was — the wedding-clothes provided." But among her children was a poor crippled boy, who had been allowed full swing ever since the death of his father. "Georgie," said the mother, calling him to her, "Georgie, I am going to do something pretty soon that I should like to have a little talk with you about." "Well, ma, what is it?" "I am going to marry Dr. Jones in a few days, and I hope——" "Bully for you, ma! *Does Dr. Jones know it?*" Who that wears a cap would not sympathize with that poor widow?

No. 30. But children are soothsayers and prophets; and they have open visions, it may be, if we would but listen to their low breathing. "Father," said a little Swedish girl, one still, starry night, after a long silence, "father, I have been thinking if the wrong side of heaven is so beautiful, what must the right side be?" Was not this a revelation? and such a revelation, too, that even her father must have been astonished? Was it not as if her whole character had been revealed to him, on her way upward, as by a flash from the empyrean?

No. 31. But we must be patient with all anxious inquirers. In a small Western village, there was a store kept by a nice young woman, who was a teacher in the Sabbath-school, and deeply interested in all that concerned that institution.

"Do you go to the Sabbath-school?" said she, one day, to a dirty little chap, who came blundering through the establishment, as if he had taken it for the play-ground.

"Sabbath-school! what's that?" said he.

"Don't you know? Why, a Sabbath-school is where we read in the Bible, and learn all about God, and our blessed Saviour, and the ——"

"O," said he, "I've read about God, and *t'other feller that killed his brother*, in the School Reader. Tain't no use my goin' to school Sunday; I know all about 'em." Whereupon the young lady teacher "dried up" — wilted, perhaps — and set her trap for another young reprobate.

No. 32. "A little three-year-old," says a neighbor, "was in the habit of helping himself to crackers without leave, by lifting the lid of a tin box, and plunging his little arm in up to the elbow. One day, after listening to stories about rats, he went after a cracker, and hearing a noise that he fancied was made by rats, he scampered back to the sitting-room, with big eyes and a flushed face, and assured his mother that he wasn't afraid. 'O, muzzer!' said he, 'I ain't afaid o' *wats, but I'se so tired*

I couldn't lift the cover!'" How many grown people have you heard guilty of a similar subterfuge. Not afraid, to be sure — not they — but only somewhat hurried, or having just remembered an engagement, as they were about lifting the lid of something dangerous.

No. 33. And here is a case of downright special pleading, worthy of Lord Coke himself, or Saunders, or Theophilus Parsons, or Chitty, or Judge Gould. "Oh, Tommy, that was abominable in you, to eat your little sister's share of the cake!" "Didn't you tell me, ma, that I was always to *take her part?*" said Tommy.

No. 34. "George," said a minister to one of the little boys, who looked as if butter wouldn't melt in his mouth, "where is your sister Minnie?" "Gone to heaven, sir." "What! — is she dead?" "O, no, sir; she went to buy a box of matches." "Why, you said she had gone to heaven." "Yes, sir — but you said last Sunday that matches were made in heaven, and so I thought she went there."

N. B. — I don't believe a word of this; but if true, all I have to say is, that, like the princes in the tower, it is well that such children are not often allowed to grow up. "Whom the gods love die young," said the ancients; but I say, Whom the gods love die of old age — unless they have been snuffed out for their untimely brilliancy.

No. 35. "Father, I don't like the bishop." "Why, dear?" "Because he sprinkled water all over my new frock, and said '*Fanny, I despise thee!*'"

No. 36. A little girl of seven years, who had been brought up to go to *meeting*, and knew nothing about a church, high or low, was taken by a friend to the Episcopal church on communion day. Returning home, she was asked by her father how she liked the service. "Well, papa," she answered, "I must say that I don't like to go to a place where the minister *has to change his shirt three times in meeting.*" Ritualistic, High-Church ceremonies, the young lady was not quite prepared for.

No. 37. A certain little Sissy, being worried by a big brother till she was out of all patience, plumped down upon her knees, where she stood, and cried out, "O Lord! bless my brother Tom. He lies — he steals — he swears; all boys do — we girls don't. Amen!" Was the poor thing a little pharisee in her indignation, without knowing it? or was she only — like most of us who are loudest in our outcries for the salvation of others — a little overburdened with self-righteousness?

No. 38. *Small boy on tip-toe to his playfellows.* — "Now you hush there, all of you."

"Why, what's the matter, Bobby?" "Well — we've got a new baby. It's very weak and tired, and walked all the way from heaven last night; and you mustn't be kicking up a row here now."

No. 39. *Little Tommy.* — "I say, ma, is it true that we are made out of the dust?"

Ma. — "Yes, Tommy; so we are told."

Tommy. — "I'll be hanged if I can believe it; 'cause you see, if we was, when we sweat, wouldn't we be muddy?"

That boy was a Transcendentalist, and no mistake.

No. 40. *Natural affection betraying itself.* — A man of influence and character was dying slowly of consumption. Being satisfied that his days were numbered — his very breathings counted — he used to call his little son to the bed-side, the pet of the household, and say to him, whenever he wanted any little thing done, that by and by, after he was dead and buried, the horse and carriage, and money-box, would all be little Sammy's. At last the father died, and the little fellow, then about five years of age, — with his grandfather and mother, were about leaving the graveyard, — snatched the reins from his grandfather, and sung out, "*Get up, old hoss! You's mine now, carriage, money-box and all!*" Had he been a few years older, he would have kept the secret to himself, and peradventure looked sorrowful over the untimely inheritance.

No. 41. Little Frank had been told to believe that we are all made of dust. One day, as he stood watching at the window, while a strong wind was whirling the dust into eddies, and hurrying it away into holes and corners, and there piling it up with the dried leaves, his mother asked him what he was thinking of. "O," said he, with uncommon seriousness for so young a philosopher, "I thought the dust looked as though there was going to be another little boy."

No. 42. A very little chap, who would no more have thought of going to bed without saying his prayers, than of going to bed without his supper, while the goodies were in sight, had just bidden everybody good-night, with a warm, loving kiss. That very day his mother had been teaching him the lines, "You'd scarce expect one of my age," and so he began his little prayer in the following fashion: "Now I lay me down to sleep, I pray the Lord my soul to keep; if I should chance to fall below Demosthenes or Cicero, don't view me with a cricket's eye, but ——"

"Hush, hush!" said his mother; "O hush, my boy! that's no part of the prayer."

"Yes it is too, mamma — don't view me with a cricket's eye," etc., etc.

Didn't that mother laugh a little to herself, think you? I'll bet she did.

No. 43. A teacher in one of our Sabbath-schools, who had quite a reputation for accommodating his lesson to the understanding of children, said to a little bit of a thing, one day, with whom she had been laboring for a long while, "If a naughty girl should strike you, my dear, you would forgive her, wouldn't you?" "Yeth, marm — if I couldn't catch her," was the reply — only to be matched by the dying Highlander, who called out to a neighboring chief, whom he had just been reconciled to, "But mark ye, lairdee — mind now — if I get abroad agen, all this goes for naethin'."

No. 44. Another little chap, just verging upon three, but of a thoughtful, prying disposition far beyond his years, sat watching his mother while she was making biscuit for tea — though her husband was an Orthodox clergyman of Pittsfield, Mass. — and asked her if it was not wicked to work on Sunday. "Certainly," said she. "O my!" said he, clapping his little hands, "won't 'oo catch it, when 'oo gets to heaven!"

No. 45. And then, too, how knowing the little wretches are sometimes. A young gentleman of about five summers was travelling in a crowded stage-coach, and had been taken into the lap of a passenger. On the way, some stories were told about pickpockets and their adroitness, and the conversation at last became general. "Ah, my fine fellow," said the gentleman who had the little one upon his knee, "how easy I could pick *your* pocket"— as it lay gaping near his hand. "No you couldn't, neither," said the boy, "'cause I've been looking out for you all the way."

No. 46. And how wise beyond their

years, and how full of resource in danger, sometimes. As three children, Peter Mitchell, Louis Leach, and Ann I. Lindsay, aged eight, five and four — I give their names, that they be remembered, and the facts verified — were playing about the premises of Mr. Horace Balcomb, in the town of Sudbury, Mass., Leach tumbled into a hogshead of rain-water set in the earth, five feet deep. As soon as he fell in, the boy Mitchell ran away to find his mother, who lived a long way off; but the little girl — only four, you will remember — managed to get hold of the drowning boy by the shoulders, and keep his head above the water, till the neighbors came to her help, and pulled him out in safety.

No. 47. In a Boston Sunday-school — where, of course, impertinent, puzzling questions are never allowed — the teacher asked,

"Where was Jesus *taken*, when he was arrested in the garden?" A bright little thing answered immediately, "To the station-house." Whereupon the teacher observed that there were no station-houses at that time; and the poor child instantly corrected herself by saying, "I meant the State's Prison." Teachers, beware!

No. 48. A naughty little boy, being told by his mother that God would not forgive him, if he did something, answered, "Yes He would too — God likes to forgive little boys — that's what He's for." Of course that boy was a Universalist from the shell, and had about as clear a notion of what God was *for*, as many a profound theologian, or metaphysician.

No. 49. But we have Grace Darlings, Florence Nightingales, and many other self-denying, self-sacrificing heroines in miniature. We have only to look about us, and have our ears open, and see, and hear, and remember for ourselves, that female wonders are of all ages and every age, and that God never measures them by feet or inches, nor counts their years, nor weighs them in any other than the scales with which He weighed the earth itself, at the beginning.

A long train of cars, fourteen or fifteen at least, were hurrying through the Alleghanies. They were crowded with passengers. As they went headlong down the inclined plane, they came to a short, narrow curve, hewed through the living rock, with a high, steep wall on each side. Suddenly a steam-whistle was heard through the gorge, screaming, Put on the brakes! put on the brakes! Every window flew up, and scores of heads were thrust out, and all the passengers sprang to their feet, while the cars went thundering on, with a continually increasing speed. As the engine approached the curve, the engineer had caught a glimpse of a little girl playing on the track with her baby-brother. One moment! and the cars would be tearing over them. The scream of the whistle startled the little girl, and her marvellous readiness and self-possession, like a flash. Seizing her baby-brother, she crowded him into a crevice made by blasting, and just about large enough to admit the little fellow; and the next moment, while the passengers were holding their breath, and expecting to see the poor girl crushed against the steep wall, they heard a clear, sweet, childish voice, like one crying in the wilderness, "Cling close to the rock, Johnny! cling close to the rock!" and saw the baby cuddling up close to the rough wall, as to the bosom of its mother, while the ponderous cars whirled past him like a tornado.

Careless for herself, or at the worst, not thinking at all of herself, the poor little barefooted sister stood for a moment like her brother's guardian-angel, between the living and the dead.

No. 50. But just read the following, which is undoubtedly true — true in every particular. Three children belonging to New Brunswick got lost in the woods. It was a dreary, wild region; a dark storm was brewing; it was near nightfall. The eldest, only six, having satisfied herself that there was no hope of their being found, nor of their finding their way out before the next day, put the little ones into a sheltered nook, stripped off most of her own clothes to wrap them in, and went away in search of dry sea-weed and brush, to cover them with. The next day the little ones were found all warm and breathing, with the sea-grass and brush heaped up about them, and the dear little six-year-old mother lying dead and stiff on the shore, alongside of the last pile of brush she had gathered, but wanted the strength to carry off.

No. 51. Three little girls were playing among the poppies and sage-brush of the back-yard. Two of them were making believe keep house, a little way apart, as near neighbors might. At last one of them was overheard saying to the youngest of the lot, "There now, Nellie, you go over to Sarah's house and stop there a little while, and talk as fast as ever you can, and then you come back and tell me what she says about me, and then I'll talk about her; and then you go and tell her all I say, and then we'll get mad as hornets, and won't speak when we meet, just as our mothers do, you know; and that'll be such fun — won't it?" Hadn't these little mischiefs lived to some purpose? and were they not close observers, and apt scholars, charmingly trained for the chief business of life in a small neighborhood?

No. 52. A young hopeful of our acquaintance, under five years of age, has been for a long time debating with himself whether he would be a circus-rider or a brigadier-general. After weighing all the *pros* and *cons*, he has decided for the circus. What a pity some of our brigadiers had not gone through a similar process in the late war — and arrived at the same conclusion! We should have been spared many a blundering mishap.

No. 53. A three-year-old baby in Georgetown, D. C., having watched the operations of newsboys and letter-carriers while distributing circulars, newspapers, etc., took from his father's desk a large pile of business letters, and began the process of distribution with astonishing success; but, after all, brought no blushes to anybody's cheek, so far as we have reason to believe, notwithstanding the example set him by the little boy with his sister's love-letters, already mentioned. See No. 20.

Well do I remember a little chubby fellow strutting through the country kitchen of his father, when I myself was but a broth of a boy, with a heap of folded papers sticking out of his trousers' pocket. "These be all writs, by George!" said he, slapping his thigh as he went along. Upon further inquiry, we found that he was imitating a new deputy-sheriff, who used to come a-courting there Sabba'-days.

No. 54. A young gentleman of only six at the outside, was cruelly beset by a baby of eighteen months, with decided manifestations of fondness. "Don't you see, Johnny, that the baby wants to kiss you?" said his mother. "Yes 'm — 'at's 'cause he tates me for his papa," was the explanation of Lilliput. My own little fellow used to complain that the servant-girls were always under his feet, when he invaded the kitchen.

No. 55. While crossing a steam-ferry, a little three-year-old exclaimed, as he saw a sail-boat, "O, mamma! there's a boat with a bonnet on" — a poke-bonnet, of course.

No. 56. And sometimes the best of us get more than we have bargained for, while trying to enlighten these will-o'-the-wisps. A preacher, who was talking to the boys in a pleasant, familiar way at the New-Hampshire State Reform-School, about good people being respected while the naughty were despised and shunned, ventured on an illustration suited to their capacities. "Now, boys, when

I walk through the streets, and I speak to some people, and not to others, what is the reason?" "'Cause some are rich and some are poor," yelped a little fellow in the corner; who, it may be, never heard of the Apostle James, nor of what he says in Chapter II. about the rich man coming into your assembly with a gold ring, in goodly apparel, and also a poor man in vile raiment, and you say to the first, "Sit thou here in a good place; and to the poor, Stand thou there, or sit under my footstool;" yet was he learned in the Scripture nevertheless, and that without knowing it, — God Almighty being his teacher.

No. 57. Can this be true? If yea, that child must have died young. It is from the *Lawrence Eagle.* "In a gentleman's family in this city," says the editor, "there is a little boy somewhat remarkable for smartness, and for his understanding of 'pure English undefiled.' He is only four. Not many days since, he was at the table 'cutting up' in the usual way, when his mother reproved him. Upon this he began buttering a huge slice of bread at such a furious rate, that his mother found it necessary to interfere again: 'Why Johnny,' said she, 'how you do behave! You mustn't eat so much butter; it will be the death of you.' The little chap looked up with a roguish smile, and said, 'Well, mother, I mean to go well buttered, you see, if I am not so well *bread*.'" This the editor was kind enough to explain, by enclosing "*bred*" in a parenthesis, after the style of newspaper purveyors, who seem to take it for granted that most of their capital jokes are unintelligible to the common reader.

No. 58. Little Daisy's mother was trying to make her understand the meaning of *smile*. "Oh yes, I know," said the little one, her face all lighting up as she spoke, "it is the whisper of a laugh." Quite equal to the "frozen music" of architecture, or the "poetry of motion." *Sed quære,* as the lawyers say, Was such a thing ever said by a little child? I trow not.

No. 59. But here is something we can believe. A buxom Ohio school-girl was going through her calisthenic performances for the amusement of her little brothers and sisters. A youthful visitor, full of compassion for the poor thing, asked her brother *if that gal had fits?* "No," replied the indignant brother, "them's gymnastics." "Oh, I see; how long has she had 'em?" which reminds me that I was once asked by a laborer, who saw half a hundred stout fellows exercising in the open air, bare-headed, with their jackets off, in Vœlker's London Gymnasium at St. John's Wood, "How much we got a day?"

No. 60. But the inquisitiveness of these folks, who are to govern the world hereafter, is not confined to every-day investigations; and well for us that they are not: and well must it be for the nations—for what our children are now, that will our country be hereafter.

"Mamma, how does God born people black?" said a sprightly little whippersnapper, who had been listening to a talk about the freedmen.

"By His great power."

"Well, I guess He must have a great big pot of blackin', and then He smooches 'em all over, jess as soon as they are borned."

"No, no, my dear — that would soon rub off," said mamma.

After a while a very earnest, exulting little voice was heard from underneath the bedclothes, saying, "I know now, mamma! He mixes the blackin' with the dust."

Set down that child for a thorough-going investigator — never to be put off with anything short of demonstration — like Sir Humphrey Davy, or Faraday.

No. 61. And then, too, how jealous they are of their little prerogatives, and how they stand up for themselves, when hard pushed! A returned Californian found the baby he had left in her mother's lap, a smart little wayward minx of five summers. One day he happened to offend her ladyship, when she exclaimed, "There now! I do wish you'd never married into the family."

No. 62. Freddy, a sunny-haired little fellow, just beginning to say "I shall be five next year about this time," after sitting awhile as if lost in thought, broke out with, "Say, pa, can God do anything?" "Yes, dear." "Can He make a two-year old colt in two minutes?" "Why — He wouldn't want to do that, Freddy." "But I say pa, if He did want to, could He do it?" "Yes, certainly," answered the father, somewhat annoyed at the child's pertinacity. "What! in two minutes, pa?" "Yes, in two minutes." "Well, then, the colt wouldn't be two years old, would he?" There's a logician for you — ay, and metaphysician too; but there! don't they swarm about our supper-tables and Sabbath-schools, just now, like the frogs in Egypt?

No. 63. *Putting it Home.*—A little Berkshire five-year-old began to be ravenous about bed-time, and was afraid to ask for more supper. At last, after pondering the question awhile, he said, "Mother, are little children that starve to death happy after they die?" Of course that child drew extra rations for once.

No. 64. "Sammy," said a young mother

to her darling, "Sammy dear, do you understand the difference between body and soul?" "Don't think I do, ma — that is, not exactly." "Shall mother try to make it clear to him?" "Yes, mamma." "Well, then," patting his arms and shoulders, "this is the body. The soul is what you live with; the body carries you about." "*You*, mamma — and who is you?" "Never mind now — this, as I told you," touching him again on the shoulders and arms, "this is the body; but there is something underneath, something deeper in. You can feel it now. What is it?" "O, I know!" said he, with a flash of delighted intelligence overspreading every feature, "it is my flannel undershirt." Of course it was! What other soul had he any idea of after mamma was done with him?

No. 65. *O Hush!* — A gentleman was admiring the beautiful hair of a young, handsome, fashionable widow, when her little girl, who had no idea of being overlooked, observed, with a fling and a pout, "I guess my hair would look well too, if I took as much care of it. Mamma never sleeps in her hair." Of course pollywog took a lesson, after bed-time, with the young ladies who "tingle, skeem, an' dance."

No. 66. A clergyman of astonishing pertinacity, having tired out a large congregation long before he had reached his tenthly, stopped to take breath and wipe the sweat from his forehead, and was just beginning afresh, when a little miss, just under the pulpit, exclaimed, "O mother! he aint a-goin' to stop at all! he is a-swellin' up again."

No. 67. A fine manly little fellow of five years tumbled on the door-step and cut his upper lip, so that a surgeon had to sew it up. He sat in his mother's lap during the operation, pale and speechless, though large tears gathered in his eyes, and seemed just ready to fall. "O dear!" said she, as the doctor finished off, "I'm afraid it will leave a bad scar." "Never mind," said Charley, patting her on the cheek, "never mind, mother, darling, my mustache will cover it!"

There's a hero for you. How much better than Nelson's "Kiss me, Hardy."

No. 68. A boy who was warmly praised for not having once taken his eyes off the preacher, answered, in the honesty of his little heart, "O, I only wanted to see how near he was to the end."

No. 69. A Sandusky mother—was she a gipsy?—so runs the little story, was reproving her three-year-old perplexity for eating icicles. "I didn't eat 'em, mamma," said he, "I only sucked the juice out of 'em." Worthy of any bar on earth, and of almost any special pleader in politics or law, metaphysics or political economy.

No. 70. "The little darling! It didn't strike neighbor Smith's poor little baby a-purpose, did he? It was a mere accident, wasn't it, dear?" "Yes, mamma, to be sure it was, an' if he don't behave himself an' stop makin' mouths at me, I'll crack him again."

No. 71. "Well Susie, how do you like your school?" "O, ever so much, papa." "That's right, Susie. And now tell me what you have learned to-day?" "Well, papa, I've learned the names of all the little boys."

And what more would you have? though the young lady were at a boarding-school, and learning the polka, and the waltz, or the schottische?

No. 72. "I say, my fine fellow, where's this road go to?" "It hain't ben nowhere sence we've lived in these parts." A legal question put to a witness on the stand, legally answered — hey?

No. 73. "I do wish you would behave!" said a boy to his little sister, in a fit of impatience. "Don't speak so to your sister," said mamma, "she is a good little girl on the whole." "I don't see where the *a good* comes in," he replied. "It comes in right after the *a*," said the little bepraised. Wasn't she smart? — or "just as cunnin' as she *could* be?"

No. 74. "What did you use to do, mamma, before you was married?" asked a little cherub, not four years old. "Well, my dear, I had a very good time, generally." "A good time!" he exclaimed with a look of astonishment, "what! without me?" Such babies will never allow themselves to be undervalued, even to the last. They *will be missed*, if they are not *mastered*. Not so bad — hey?

No. 75. A gentlewoman — I hate ladies — belonging to Gardiner, Maine, paid a visit to the graveyard with her little daughter. Seeing the effigy of a horse on one of the upright slabs, she stooped down to read the inscription, but nothing did she find to explain the mystery; whereupon the child whispered, that "maybe the poor man died of *nightmare.*" A very plausible conjecture, was it not, for a region where so many live and die of the same ailment? now under the name of apoplexy, and now under that of the heart disease, or plethora?

No. 76. A little creature, under three years of age, on being told that she was too little to have a muff, asked, with a bright flush over her whole face, "Am I too little to be cold?" Another, on being refused admission to the church, upon the ground that she was too young, asked if she was too young to sin and be sorry for it?

No. 77. Another three-year-old, on returning from her first visit to church, asked for a cup of water, that she might christen her doll, just as the preacher did the baby. And why not — if mother had failed to enlighten her upon the subject of infant baptism?

No. 78. Two little girls, both under six, were overheard in conversation about their neighbors. "Emma," said one of them, "wouldn't it be awful if somebody should up and shoot our school-mistress?" "Yes indeed," was the reply; "but then, wouldn't it be nice not to have any school?"

No. 79. A little boy once asked a godly minister, "Do you think my father will go to heaven?" "Yes," replied the minister. "Well then, *I* tell *you*, if he can't have his own way there, he won't stay long, you bet."

No. 80. *Tit for Tat.* — The family were

at dinner. The conversation turned upon a trip to the islands, about to take place. A clergyman spoke to the little one, and after some bantering, asked her if she could say the alphabet backward. "No sir," said she, wondering what next, as the tadpole did when his tail dropped off. "Then," said he, "you can't go to the islands." After looking very thoughtful for a few moments, she asked, "Can you say the Lord's Prayer backward?" "No, my dear." "Then," said she, "you can't go to heaven." Was not the inference honest and fair, granting the premises?

No. 81. A little blue-eyed maiden, who was romping with her fifth Christmas doll, and listening to some conversation about unhappy marriages, incompatibilities of temper, and the Chicago recipe for unmarrying, turned to her mother and said, "Well, ma, I'm never going to marry. I'm going to be a widow." The dear little chatterbox! If she could only have kept her own counsel a few years longer. How many are there who would like being widows, without going through the form of marriage? but then, they'll never say so, for widows have their privileges, and privileges, too, that wives have not.

No. 82. And here we have something out of the common way, well vouched for, and thoroughly safe to be repeated. A little boy of only eight years, a son of Mr. Elias Bates, drove to the Agricultural Fair in Medford, Mass., a pair of black calves, which were so perfectly trained as to draw a little blue wagon, which had been got up for the occasion. The little fellow — and this, probably, will be thought the best part of the story by most of our young readers, — was furnished with *scrip* from the wallets of the bystanders to the amount of nobody knows how many dollars; enough, at any rate, to nearly fill his cap. Whereat, says the narrator, he was so entirely overcome with surprise and joy, that he cried, and laughed, tried to talk, and then fairly broke down, and took to his heels, and ran away, as if the dogs were after him.

No. 83. Lilly and Nina had prepared a doll's breakfast, and arrayed it on a sideboard, while they went to take a romp in the garden. Master Bob, their little brother, clambered up the side-board and began gobbling the dainties, as boys will do, you know, whatever may be their age. "Why, Bobby!" said his mother, looking in at the open door, "what *are* you doing there?" "Playin' pussy, mamma."

No. 84. At a country fair in New Jersey, not long ago, a little boy who was running about, like a distracted thing, and bawling as if he would split his throat, was asked what was the matter. "I want my mammy," said he, "that's what's the matter! Didn't I tell the darned thing she'd lose me?"

No. 85. A little four-year-old went to church in Bridgeport, Connecticut, last summer. On getting home, her mother asked her if she remembered the text. "O yes, mamma; it was this: 'The Ladies Sewing Circle will meet at Mrs. So-and-so's house, on Monday afternoon.'" A capital text, whatever may have been the sermon.

No. 86. A Boston boy, five years of age, and a type of many now flourishing there, if not a type of that class who are to be the gold-brokers of hereafter, at least a representative boy of the shrewd and calculating, now on their way up in the cashier-business, which so often ends of late in there being neither cash-*here* nor cash-*there* for stockholders, having stolen, or appropriated, a can of milk, was taken solemnly to task for the misdemeanor by his loving mother. "What on earth were you going to do with the milk?" said she. "O, I was going to steal a little puppy to drink it," was the reply. Perfectly satisfactory, no doubt, like certifying checks by the handful, and appropriating, or *conveying*, the gold of widows and orphans by the wheelbarrow-load into a friend's pocket, or in speculating where what you gain is yours, and what you lose, another's.

No. 87. A clergyman asked some children why we say Our Father *who art in Heaven*, since God is everywhere? A little drummer-boy, who stood afar off, looked as if he understood the question. "Well, my little soldier, what have you to say?" "Because it's head-quarters," he replied.

No. 88. "A little nephew of ours," says a contributor, "went with his sister to school not long ago, for the first time. They kept him there five mortal hours, with a short recess, which he did not know how to take advantage of. On being asked how he enjoyed the school, he answered, 'Petty well, I tank you, but I dut awfully *rested.*'"

No. 89. *A Specimen of Childish Faith, which, if not dwarfed nor blighted, would be enough — almost — to move Mountains, after getting its growth.* — Two little girls, one nine and the other eleven, on getting up one morning, had a trial to see which would get dressed first. Little Sue was the winner; and turning to her sister, with the triumphant air of a victor at the Olympian games, she said, "I knew I should beat you, Sissy; for I asked God to help me, *and I knew He would.*"

No. 90. A fine-looking, saucy, high-spirited girl of ten, bought of a fashionable shoemaker a pair of warranted boots. They broke out with one day's wear. She carried them back to him. After turning them over, inside and out, awhile, he said, "They were not taken in quite enough, I see." "No," she replied, "but I was."

No. 91. A promising little chap having heard it stated confidentially that a neighbor was married, and that she had a little boy and girl, stowed the fact away for future use; and not long after reproduced it in a large company of ladies and gentlemen, after this fashion: "Miss M——, I tink our tortus-shell tat's ben dittin married — she's dut tittens." But tortoise-shell cats don't have kittens — at least, not of themselves, if by proxy; but *qui facit per alium facit per se*, as the lawyers say; and the little boy may have misunderstood the symptoms.

No. 92. Charley, the other day, on seeing three or four funerals in swift succession, expressed a wish that he might die "before Heaven was too full."

No. 93. A mother, out a-shopping with her little girl and boy, bought him a rubber balloon, which escaped while he was playing with it, and went off up into the sky. Sissy, on seeing the tears in his eyes, and his quivering chin, said, "Never mind, Neddy — when you dies and dose to Heaben, you'll dit it."

No. 94. A Bible-class had been called upon for the names of the precious stones mentioned in the Scriptures. After the question had gone through the class, one little fellow held up his hand. "Well, Tommy," said the teacher, "what precious stone have you found?" "Brimthtone, thir!"

No. 95. This beautiful anecdote must be given in the very words of the narrator: "A lady visiting New York, found a ragged, cold, and hungry child gazing wistfully at some cakes in a shop window. She took the little forlorn thing by the hand, led her into the shop, bought her a cake, and then led her away, and supplied her other wants. The grateful little creature looked her full in the face, and whispered, '*Are you God's wife?*'"

No. 96. A fashionable woman called upon a dentist to have some teeth filled, taking with her a little niece. Among these were two front incisors, which were filled on the lower edge. In a pleasant mood, when everything went well with Aunty, glimpses of the gold were occasionally seen. "O Aunt Mary," said the child, "how I should like to have copper-toed teeth, like yours!"

And this reminds me of a little boy, whose father was bald-headed. One day he was sent to have his hair cut. "How would you like to have it cut, my little man?" said the artist. "Like papa's, with a hole in the top," said he, — perhaps to see through.

No. 97. Master Jimmy was standing on his father's steps, in broad daylight, smoking a cigar. "Why, Jim," said a neighbor, who was hurrying by, "when did you learn to smoke?" "O," says the boy — "when I was a little fellow!"

No. 98. "Papa," said a small urchin with a mischievous eye — "I say, papa, ought the master to flog a fellar for what he didn't do?" "Certainly not, my boy." "Well, then, he flogged me to-day when I didn't do my sum." And there he had him!

No. 99. And this, too, is vouched for — though not by me: A little girl, about five years old, heard a preacher vociferating in prayer till the roof rang again. "Mother," said the little one, "don't you think, if he lived nearer to God, he wouldn't have to pray so loud?" Maybe she had been told about the priests of Baal, and their shouting before the Hebrew prophet, who mocked them.

No. 100. Bishop Simpson, they say, in a lecture delivered at Boston, had the courage to say, that in two or three years, at furthest, Chinese servants would be common there. Next morning the father happened to mention it. "O, pa," whispered Minnie, "won't it be nice! we shall have a Chinese servant, and she will eat all the rats, and so we sha'n't have to keep a cat!"

No. 101. A youngster, who had been playing in a mud-puddle till his rubber boots were full of the dirty water, came home at last to report progress, and ask leave to sit again. But his mother, with an eye to doctor's bills, and a whooping-cough, or scarlet fever, said No; and the child was kept in the house all day, till he could bear it no longer. "O mamma!" said he, at last, "please whip me, and let me go out again — *do.*" It seems that he had outwaded all the rest of the boys, without going much beyond his depth.

No. 102. Children are wonders. No matter how well acquainted with them we may be, they are always taking us off our feet. A pious woman heard a child, as she thought, say — and the child, too, of godly parents — "Dam it to hell — who buys?" — having a basket on his arm, containing she knew not what, so shocked was she. On reporting the case at head-quarters, the affair was investigated, and it turned out that the poor little fellow had a bushel of damsons, which he made believe hawk round, after the fashion of small dealers who cry their wares in the street. What he tried to say was, "Damsons to sell — who buys?"

No. 103. "How many sisters did you say, my dear?" "Only one beside myself." "And how many brothers?" "None at all." "What! no brother!" "No sir; mamma don't *approve* of boys." That's a fact.

No. 104. A little nigger-boy at the South had just been equipped with a new suit of clothes, the first he ever had in his life, you may be sure. Next morning he appeared with one leg of the trousers ripped up from shoe to waistband. On being asked how it happened, he answered, "Please ma'am, I wanted to hear it *flop!*"

No. 105. Another little boy, while playing by himself on the carpet, burst out with a ringing laugh. On being questioned, it turned out that he had taken off the tail of a little toy pony, and stuck it into the pony's mouth. "Papa," said he, "do Dod see everything?" "Yes, my boy." "Well, then, I dess Dod will laugh, when He sees my pony."

No. 106. "I have somewhere met with a story," says a pleasant, gossiping observer, "about a man who went, one dark night, to steal corn from his neighbor's patch. He had taken his little boy with him to keep watch. The man jumped over the fence with a large bag on his arm; but before he began to fill it, he stopped and looked about on all sides, and, not seeing anybody, was just going to work, when his little boy cried out, 'Oh, father, father! there is one way you haven't looked yet!'

"The old man was rather startled, and asked what he meant.

"'Why,' said the little one, 'you forgot *to look up.*'

"The father was silent — thunderstruck — as if he had been admonished by a little guardian angel: he went back to the fence, took his little boy by the hand, and hurried away without the corn."

No. 107. A mother was reading to her child, a boy of seven, about another little boy whose father had lately died, leaving the family destitute, whereupon the boy went to work for himself, and managed to support them all.

"Now, my little man," said mother, after she had finished the story, "if papa should be taken away, wouldn't you like to help your poor mother and your little sisters?"

"Why, ma — what for? Ain't we got a good house to live in?"

"O yes, my child; but we couldn't eat the house, you know."

"Well — ain't we got flour and sugar, and other things in the store-room?"

"Certainly, my dear; but they wouldn't last long — and what then?"

"Well — ain't there enough to last, till you could get another husband?"

Mamma *dried up* — just as the boy had *slopped over*.

No. 108. A mother had been telling her little girl about the blessings above. "But will mamma be there too?" asked the child. "Yes; you and I, and little brother, and papa." "O no, mamma," said she — "papa can't go; papa can't leave the store."

No. 109. A little four-year-old, living just out of New York, was saying the Lord's Prayer at his mother's knee. After he had finished, she said to him —

"Now, Sandy, ask God to make you a good boy."

The child hesitated, grew thoughtful, and, after a few minutes, looked up and whispered —

"It's no use, mamma — He won't do it, I tell you; I've asked Him ever so many times."

No. 110. A little girl, the daughter of a Brooklyn wife, had been listening to an argument about the occupations above, and the great Hereafter. Turning suddenly to her aunt, she asked what people found to do after they went to Heaven. Her aunt, being taken by surprise, answered, "O, they play on golden harps." "What — all the time!" "Yes — all the time, dear." "Then," said the child, "I don't want to go there — I should be *so* tired; and, what is more, I don't like the music."

No. 111. "Is it still raining, my dear?" said a mother to her child of only three, at Jamaica, L. I. The child, after looking out of the window, turned to her mother and said, "No, mamma, it ain't a-rainin' now, but the trees is leakin'." The same child, having a habit of putting pins in her mouth, was anxiously watched. Whenever she was very still, they knew she was in some mischief. The other day, on seeing her stand at the bureau in perfect silence, her mother began to have her suspicions. "Mary," said she, "you are playing with pins, I'm afraid; I hope you haven't got any in your mouth." "I ain't dut any in my mouth now," she said; "but I bin playin' pins is meat."

No. 112. One round more, and I throw up the sponge. The same little wee thing — a granddaughter of my own, by the way, and the first of the series — mentioned in No. 10, who spelled *pigeon* with *Q. U. A. I. L.*, and pronounced it *fidget*, was looking at a hive, in a book for babies. "O," she shouted — "O, grandpa, I know what them is! They's the honeys, and when they go away, I mean to steal their *porridge*." N. B. — She had always called honey porridge.

No. 113. Once — and I give this for a fine illustration of the total depravity we hear so much of — I had a pleasant specimen of the inward working of that self-reproach we are all tried with sometimes, in this way: Miss Nellie seemed shy of me one morning, when she came into the breakfast room. Instead of running up to grandpa with a kiss upon her little red lips, she kept aloof, and went wandering about beyond my reach, with her eyes fastened on me all the time. At last, unable to bear it longer, she whimpered, "Oo needn't look at me so, grandpa; I ony toot one tawbelly."

No. 114. "High, there, high!" said Grandfather Hall to my little boy — the first we had. "You don't know where you are." "Yes I do, grandpa." "Well, where are you?" "I'm here," was the reply.

No. 115. *Analogy.*—"What the plague is that?" said a father to his little boy, as a dog ran past them with a muzzle over his head. "Well, I guess it's a little *hoop-skirt*," said the boy.

No. 116. *Prepare to Pucker!*—A little

four-year-old chap had been trying a long while to pucker his mouth into shape, for whistling a national tune, which he had just heard upon the street. At last he gave it up, and went to his mother with tears in his eyes, exclaiming, "Ma, I's so little I tan't make a hole big enough for Yankee Doolum to dit out."

No. 117. *Disinterested Advice.*—"Mammy!" said another little fellow, just big enough to gobble dough-nuts, and relish mud-pies and lollipop, who had been set to rocking the cradle of his baby brother, of whom he professed to be very fond — *very* — "Mammy! if the Lord's got any more babies to give away, don't you take 'em."

No. 118. *Rather a Paradox.*—"What is conscience?" asked a sabbath-school teacher. "An inward monitor," was the reply of a smart little fellow, not large enough to spell ratiocination with safety. "And what is a monitor?" "One of the iron-clads." Ergo.

No. 119. *The Reason why.* — A boy of nine, having a motherly hen with a large brood of chickens to watch, undertook to satisfy his mother that he would rather be a chicken than a boy — chickens were so much happier. The mother was obstinate, and so was the boy; but the next day he happened to come across a copy of "Don Quixote," with which he was so carried away, that he ran off to his mother to tell her that, on the whole, "he guessed he'd rather be a boy than a chicken;" for, "if I was a chicken," said he, "I couldn't read 'Don Quixote.'"

No. 120. *Retribution.*—A little four-year-old shaver, living on Munjoy, had picked up some naughty words — nobody knew where. But his mother, to cure him, was in the habit of touching the tip of his tongue with a little black pepper, until he seemed to have abandoned the practice. Only last week, however, the Old Adam broke out afresh, and he ran off to his mother, saying, "Dod dam it! Dod dam it! Now dit your pepper-bots!" and then rushed to the table and grabbed the box, and turned it up for the prescribed allowance; but the cover came off — as might have been expected — filling his mouth, so that he could neither speak nor breathe for awhile, and looked upon it as a judgment, and has now left off swearing — for the present.

No. 121. *Influence of Example.*—"I've done it, mamma! I've done it!" screamed a little three-year-old tantrybogus, from the top of the cellar stairs, to his mother, who had just left the kitchen for a few minutes. "Tum and tee, mamma!" And sure enough, he had *done it!* having upset a basket of eggs, and smashed them all, one after another, in a sort of ecstacy. His mother had been preparing for a batch of cake, and he had been delighted with her treatment of the eggs.

No. 122. *Appropriate Language.* — "Auntie," said another little three-year-old, one day — "Auntie, I don't lite mine apons tarched so drefful. So much tarchess makes the tiffness tratch my — bareness."

No. 123. *After-thoughts.* — Master Frank was in the habit of tumbling out of bed o' nights, and his father would call him to account for it next morning. One day he said, "Well, Frank, and so you tumbled out of bed again?" "No I didn't, papa — it was the pillow; for I went up to see, and the pillow was on the floor, by the bedside." "What made you cry, then, my boy?" "Well, you see, it was so dark, papa, I couldn't tell at first whether 'twas me or the pillow."

No. 124. *Baby Theologians.* — A child in the sabbath-school, on being asked if he could mention a place where God was not, answered, "He is not in the thoughts of the wicked."

Another, when told that God was everywhere, asked, "In this room?" "Yes." "In the closet?" "Yes." "In the drawers of my desk?" "Yes — everywhere — He's in your pocket now." "No He ain't, though." "And why not?" "Tauth, I ain't dut no pottet."

No. 125. *A great Mystery.*—"There is a little girl in Kentucky," says a respectable paper, judging by appearances, "who has never spoken to her father. She talks freely with anybody else, but when her father speaks to her, she is speechless. They have whipped her, again and again, but to no purpose; for she declares, with trembling lips, and with tears in her eyes, that she has often tried to speak to him, but could not."

No. 126. *Childish Metaphysics.*—A grandson of the governor of Virginia, a child of only four or five summers, was on a visit, not long ago, to his maternal grandfather, a large landholder in Ohio. One day, after a first visit to the sabbath-school, he led his grandfather down to a magnificent tree, heavily laden with walnuts.

"Grandpa," said he, "whom do all these woods and fields belong to?"—of course the child said *who*, instead of *whom;* but that is neither here nor there.

"They belong to me, Charley."

"No, sir—*no!*—they belong to God."

The grandfather said nothing, till they reached the tree.

"Well, my boy, whom does this tree belong to?" he asked, as they stopped underneath its wide, heavy branches.

For a moment, Charley hesitated; and then, looking up into the tree, he said, while his mouth watered visibly, "Well, gran'father, the tree belongs to God, but the walnuts are *ours*."

No. 127. "*A touch of Nature makes the*

whole world kin." — A little boy, who had been tormented by clouds of mosquitoes till he could bear it no longer, exclaimed, "O dear me! O dear me! I do wish God would kill the mosquitoes! I don't know what I would give Him, if He only would."

No. 128. *An Etymologist.* — A Connecticut boy insisted on knowing what was meant by the slang phrase, "a gone sucker"; and was overheard praying soon after, on being sent off to bed —"God bless papa and mamma, and baby; but I'se been such a bad boy, I rather guess I'm *a gone sucker.*"

No. 129. "How old are you, my dear?" said a railroad conductor to a little gentlewoman, whose mother was trying to pass with a half ticket. "I'm nine at home," was the reply, "but in the cars I'm only half-past six."

No. 130. *A fair Inference.* — Dear little Mamie H., who had just got over her sixth birthday, was studying her sabbath-school lesson, when her mother told her, in reply to some question she had urged with a deal of earnestness, that the naughty devil was black. "Well, then, mamma," said the child, "if he was a good devil, I s'pose he'd be white."

No. 131. *Grandchildren on their Good Behavior.*—Bishop, to Nellie peeping through the side-lights, with a big tom-cat in her arms. "Come and see me, Nellie."

"No — I tan't."

Bishop.—"Come come, and bring the cat with you; I want to see her."

"No, no! Tommy don't like Bishops."

No. 132. *A Baby Spendthrift.* — "I say, Bobby," said one little youngster to another, "lend me two cents, will yer? I got up so early, that I spent all my money 'fore breakfast."

"More fool you."

"Wal! — how should I know the day was goin' to be so long?"

No. 133. *A Maxim well applied.*— "Never put off till to-morrow, my dear boy, what you can do to-day," said a watchful mother to her inquiring son. "Yes, mamma, and so we'll have the raspberry-pie now, that's put away for to-morrow — shan't we, mamma?"

No. 134. *A fair Inference.* — At a sabbath-school concert in a crowded and popular church, the pastor, who prided himself on the quickness and cleverness of his little ones, said, "Boys, when I heard your beautiful songs to-night, I had to work hard to keep my feet still; now what do you think was the trouble with them?" "*Chilblainth!*" shouted a little chap of six, or thereabouts.

No. 135. *A timely Rebuke.*— A bright-eyed little fellow, in one of the Brooklyn private-schools, having spelt a word, was asked by his teacher, "Are you willing to bet you're right, Bennie?" The boy looked up with an air of astonishment, and replied, "I *know* I'm right, Miss V——, but I never bet."

No. 136. *A dangerous Query.*—A pupil was asked what S double E spelt. Being rather slow with his answer, the teacher grew impatient, and exclaimed, "You dunce! What is it I do with my eyes?" "O; I know the word now, ma'am — S double E, *squint.*"

No. 137. *Constructiveness.*—The Springfield Republican tells of a young gentleman who doesn't want to be the last angel God makes, because "he wants to see how He makes 'em."

No. 138. *Imitation.* — A little girl at Keokuk, Iowa, was lately found in a barn giving trapèze performances to quite a gathering of wee folks. They had fitted up a trapèze, with an old clothes-line and a broomstick, at an elevation of twenty feet. "The party was broken up," says a spectator, "before anything else was broken."

No. 139. *The Tables turned.* — "Are you talking to me, sir?" said a respectable man to a little scapegrace, who had been holding what he called an argument with his papa; "I'm your father, sir. Remember that, sir!"

"Well, who's to blame for that, I should like to know — 'taint me," said the boy.

No. 140. *Language.* — A bright, clear-eyed little thing of three summers, after listening demurely to a chapter of the Old Testament, which her father read to the family aloud one pleasant Sabbath, looked up with the air of one who felt called upon to say something, in the dead silence that followed, and whispered, "Papa, ain't God a funny fellow?" What knew that child of irreverence? What she meant to say was that she had been delighted.

No. 141. *A new Paraphrase.*—A father, who always insisted upon his children giving their version of what they heard, in their own language, to show that they understood it, asked Charlie to repeat the text which they had been listening to.

Charlie hesitated awhile, and then, as if it had come to him all at once, broke out with, "What are you loafing round here for, doin' nothing? Go into my barn-yard, and go to work, and I'll make it all right with you."

The text was, "Why stand ye here all the day idle? Go into the vineyard and work, and whatsoever is right, I will pay thee." Who will venture to say that the poor child did not understand the meaning?

No. 142. *The Darlings.* — "Mamma!"

shouted Lollipop, "make Bobby 'have himself; every time I hit him with the whapstick he hollars out."

No. 143. Another child was once heard calling out from the head of the stairs to her mamma, that nurse "wouldn't *quiet* her."

No. 144. *Tit for Tat.* — Another wee thing, after complaining of her teacher, said, with a tap of her little foot, and a something between a sob and a whimper, she did "wish Miss Maria would go to school to herself awhile, that she might see how she liked it."

No. 145. *A fair Inference.* — A little boy and girl had been repeatedly cautioned not to take the nest-egg, when foraging in the hay-mow, and along by the fences; but one evening, little Sis found her way to the nest, rather in advance of Bubby, and snatching the egg, off she started for the house. Her brother followed, screaming, "Mother!

mother! Susy's ben and got the egg the old hen measures by!"

No. 146. *Another.*—A little bit of a thing who had just got back from a party, was asked by her mamma how she had enjoyed herself. "O mamma!" said she, "I'm so full of happiness — I couldn't be no happier, without I was bigger." So reasoned Samuel Johnson. The quart pot and the pint may both be full; but the quart holds most.

No. 147. *From Over-Sea.* — A little five-year-old Parisian went to church with his mamma. Both began praying. "Mamma," whispered the little fellow, "I've said my prayer." "Say it over again, my dear." The child obeys, and whispers, "I have said it again, mamma," and gets the same answer; and so for the third time, the mother not liking to be hurried in her devotions. "But, mamma, I have said it over three times."

"Say it again, my dear." "But, mamma — won't it be tedious for the good God to listen all the time to the same prayer? What if I say over the fable I've just learnt at school?"

No. 148. *Definition of Faith.* — A child was asked, "What is faith?" "Doing God's will and asking no questions," was her reply.

Another fair Inference. — "Lottie, dear," said a little visitor to her playfellow of three, "what makes our Kitty so cross?" "'Cause she's tuttin' her teef, I spec."

No. 149. *And yet another.* — A little thing in a sabbath-school was asked by her teacher "if she always said her prayers night and morning." "No, Miss, I don't." "Why, Mary! Are you not afraid to go to sleep in the dark, without asking God to take care of you, and watch over you till morning?" "No, Miss, I ain't — 'cause I sleep in the middle."

No. 150. *Did his Best.* — A little chap

had a dirty face, and his teacher told him to go and wash it. He went away, and after a few minutes came back, with the lower part of his countenance tolerably clean, while the upper part was dirty and wet.

"Johnny," said the teacher, "why didn't you wash your face?"

"I did wash it, sir," said Johnny.

"You didn't wipe it all over, then?"

"I did wipe it, as high up as my shirt would go."

And this reminds me of a little boy who had been told never to go into the water without leave. One day he came home heated and tired, with his shirt on wrong side out. "You've been in a-swimming, Josie," said his mother. "No, mamma." "How came your shirt turned inside out, then?" "Wal," said Josie, after a moment's hesitation, "I rather guess it was when I got over that high fence, and turned a somerset, head first."

No. 151. *A new Version.*—A boy in our District School was reading a lesson from the Bible in that deliberate fashion so usual with chaps of six, and when he came to the passage, "Keep thy tongue from evil and thy lips from guile," he drawled out, with a decided emphasis, "Keep—thy—tongue from evil; and thy lips from—from—*girls.*" Of course, there followed an explosion. "Job was an oyster-man; and the Lord, he shot him with four balls," if we may believe a new reading of what was intended for Scripture: "Somebody was an *austere* man; and the Lord smote him with sore boils."

No. 152. *Children and Fools are said to speak the Truth.*—"Be you good?" said a little chap to Miss Bella M——, of the sabbath-school here.

"O no!" was the becoming reply.

"You ain't! well I knew you wasn't pretty, but I always thought you was good."

No. 153. The following sweet lines are too good for abridgment, or paraphrase. I know not where they originated; nor who was the author. Was there ever anything more childlike and beautiful than "Mamma, God knows all the rest?" — or ever lines worthier of the text?

THE UNFINISHED PRAYER.

"Now I lay"—repeat it, darling;
  'Lay me,' lisped the tiny lips
Of my daughter, kneeling, bending
  O'er her folded finger-tips.

"Down to sleep"—'To sleep,' she murmured,
  And the curly head dropped low;
"I pray the Lord"—I gently added,
  You can say it all, I know.

"'Pray the Lord'—the word came faintly,
  Fainter still—'My soul to keep;'
Then the tired head fairly nodded,
  And the child was fast asleep.

"But the dewy eyes half opened
  When I clasped her to my breast,
And the dear voice softly whispered,
  'Mamma, God knows all the rest.'"

No. 154. *Natural Language.* — A youngster of only two and a half, who had often heard complaints in the family about pegs hurting the feet, stole up to his mother one day, with his fingers in his mouth, and said, "Mamma! O mamma! Me dut pegs tummin in my mouf, and dey hurts Billy." On further examination, he was found to be cutting no less than three little teeth.

No. 155. *An embryo Theologian.* — A little boy, disputing one day with his elder sister upon some Bible question, sung out, "I tell ye, it's true! for Ma says so; an' if Ma says so, it is so, if it ain't so." That boy's career is evident enough. Submission to authority, and sheer dogmatism, will be likely to overtop the pretensions of private judgment.

No. 156. *Budding Subterfuges.* — A little girl, belonging to Hartford, Connecticut, was called to account one day by her mother for killing flies. The amusement had become a serious occupation, and her dexterity in catching them was only to be matched by her astonishing aptitude in killing them. Her mother had begun to be frightened. "Mary, my love," said she, "don't you know that God loves the little flies?"

Mary stood for a few moments, lost in thought, her beautiful countenance growing sadder and sadder, as if her conscience had begun to testify against her in a whisper, just as poor Herod's might have done, after the slaughter of *his* innocents. At last, having apparently settled the question with herself, she stole up to the nearest window where a big blue-bottle was blundering and bumping about, and buzzing at a fearful rate. After watching it for several minutes, with a piteous expression, as if her heart were too full for speech, she began whispering just loud enough to be heard by her mother, "Do ee fy know dat Dod loves oo? Duz oo love Dod?"— stretching out her little hand as if to soothe its evident terror. "Duz oo? Duz oo want to zee Dod?—well," in a tone of the tenderest commiseration, putting her finger on the fly, and crushing it softly against the glass— "Well—oo sal!"

No. 157. *A young Nero.*—And this reminds me of something told me by General Fessenden, the father of all the general Fessendens we know of. "When I was a little fellow," said he, "not more than so high, the Old Adam within me (what we Phrenologists call Destructiveness, he meant) led me to pull off the wings of flies, and to impale them on pins, and set them buzzing at the end of a hair. My father, in passing one day, stopped long enough to catch me in the act. *'Nero!'*

said he, and passed on. 'Well,' said I to myself, 'what did he mean by that? *Nero — Nero —* I'll ask somebody.' I did so — found out who Nero was, and from that day to this, have never tormented any of God's creatures! And yet, he was a lawyer, in large practice— and I believed him — that is, I believed him, till I knew better."

No. 158. *Total Depravity.* — "Do you say your prayers every day, my little man — every night and morning?" said a mother in Israel to a little reprobate of a shoe-black, to whom she had just given a trifle. "Yes 'm,— I alluz says 'em at night, mum; but any smart boy can alluz take care o' hisself in the daytime," was the reply.

No. 159. *Infant Theology.* — A visitor of large experience in sabbath-schools, asked the children at a crowded examination, "What was the sin of the Pharisees?" "Eatin' camels, ma'am," said one of the smartest, who had carried off many a prize. On further questioning, the child justified, by referring to the passage, where the Pharisees were said to strain at a gnat, and swallow a camel.

No. 160. *Sabbath-school Exercise.*—But an English gentlewoman once told me of something she herself had witnessed at a great London sabbath-school examination, where a celebrated questioner called out a little bright-eyed boy, by name, and asked him why Joseph refused to go to bed with Potiphar's wife, when she asked him. A dead silence followed, and then a look of amazement and consternation over all the house, like a cloud: "'Cause he wan't sleepy," said the boy. A dead silence followed; and then a most unseemly titter, on every side, so that the questioner's indiscretion seemed to be entirely lost sight of.

No. 161. *Effectual Prayer.* — A little boy in Jamaica went to the missionary, and told him that he had been very ill, and often wished for the minister to come and pray with him.

"But, Thomas," said the missionary, "I hope you prayed for yourself?"

"O yes, indeed!"

"Well — and how did you pray?"

"O, I jess begged."

Another child in a Sunday-school, only six at most, said, "When we kneel down here in the school-room to pray, it seems to me as if my heart was talking with God."

Another little girl, just turning four, on being questioned why she prayed to God, answered —

"Because I know He hears me, and so I love to pray to Him."

"But how do you know He hears you?"

Putting her little hand upon her heart, she whispered, "O, I know He does, mamma, because there is something here that tells me so."

No. 162. *Tit for Tat.* — A pretty four-year-old midget went out to play on the sidewalk. When she returned with wet and muddy feet, showing that she had been somewhere else, her mother began to look serious; whereupon the child, anticipating the worst, murmured, with her head in her mother's lap, "Now, mamma, you be *dood* to me, and I'll be *dood* to you."

No. 163. *A very proper Distinction.* — A little thing, not quite old enough to understand her catechism, getting puzzled over the question, "Who made you?" went for the answer to her mother. Having been told that God made her, and all her little friends, and the whole human family, she lost no time in communicating the discovery to Daisy Dean, her doll of only one summer. Taking the little one on her knee, and looking very solemn, she said, "Now, Daisy Dean, look me right in the eyes: I want to tell 'oo somesin. Dod *made* grampa — and gramma — and me — and papa and mamma; but ——" after a pause, and shaking her head slowly and impressively — "*but*, Daisy Dean, Dod only *sewed* you."

No. 164. *Human Nature.*—A boy of about five, a bagfull of bumble-bees at the best, when required to be still on the Sabbath, getting weary toward nightfall, went up to his father, who had no little of the Puritan mingled with his affection for the child, and said to him, with great seriousness, — "Come, pa, let's have some spiritual fun." This was a little too much for papa's gravity; and so he let him have it — for once.

No. 165. *Courtesy.*—" A Brooklyn friend, who believes in catechism, and teaches it with unflinching pertinacity, worthy of Calvin or Luther," says somebody — " was putting one of four through his paces one day, when the question came up, 'Who tempted Eve?' The little fellow answered, after some consideration, with a look of triumph, pointing to the floor, 'It's the gentleman that lives *down there* — I forget his name.'" For "*down there*," the reader is at liberty to substitute another phrase, if he happens not to be of the mealy-mouthed.

No. 166. *Doll-Factory.*—A preacher in the neighborhood of Lewiston had a little daughter, who had gone into the business of manufacturing paper dolls. In the midst of a sermon, lately, he drew out his pocket-handkerchief, in somewhat of a hurry, and lo! the whole air was filled with what seemed at first to be Japanese butterflies. When they settled, however, they were found to be paper dolls, about fifty in number, which had been stowed away in his pocket-handkerchief, by his little one, for safe keeping. The audience appeared to enjoy the rest of the sermon exceedingly.

No. 167. *Undiluted Orthodoxy.*—A little girl was much in the habit of reproving her dolls for misbehavior, and sometimes after a most alarming fashion. Her mother overheard her one day, while she was taking the prettiest to task for being so naughty: "O you naughty, sinful child," said she, shaking the poor little waxen image, "you'll go to the lake of fire and brimstone, you will! and you won't burn up, like other babies — you'll only jest *sizzle.*"

No. 168. *Puzzling Questions.*—A little boy, who had just been admitted to the sabbath-school, was greatly scandalized at finding, on his way home, an apothecary's shop in full blast at a neighboring corner. "But, my dear," said mamma, "the druggist is obliged to keep open Sunday, so that sick people may get medicine." "Why! do people get sick on Sunday?" "Yes, just as on any other day." "Well, good people don't die on Sunday, do they?" "Certainly." "Why, how can that be? Does heaven keep open Sunday?"

No. 169. *Childish Faith.*—The Portland Transcript knows of a little four-year-old, who, being out for a sail, was told by his mother that they were now on the sea. "On the sea, mamma! then who'll take care of us?" "God, my dear—He will take care of us." "O yes—I know—*he's one o' them kind.*"

No. 170. The same inquisitive chap could not understand how two boys who had died before he was born, could be his brothers. Mamma explained, that being her children they were his brothers, though God had taken them away to live with Him, before *he* was born. He was very silent and thoughtful for a few moments, and then exclaimed, "*O yes, I see — I used to play with 'em up there in heaven, before I came down here.*"

No. 171. *The Boy and the Bobbylink.* — A bird lighted on a twig near a little rugged-and-tough, hardly old enough to make himself understood. The child took up a stone to throw at him, after the fashion of older boys. Just then the little songster opened fire: "Bob-o'-link! bobbylink! won't you, will ye! will ye, won't you! I'll mend your breeches if you'll find the pieces—bobbylink!—link—link!" The boy's outstretched arm dropped slowly down to his side. "Why didn't you let fly, sonny?" said a stranger who had been watching him, and was not a little curious to see how the struggle would end. The boy shook his head, with a sorrowful air, but said nothing. "You might have killed him and carried him home," said the stranger.

"I touldn't," said the little scapegrace.

"Couldn't! and why not, pray?"

"'*Cause he sung so.*"

No. 172. *Superfluities.* — A youngster, on being taken to the window of a toy-shop where he saw a *papier maché* mouse, which, on being wound up, ran hither and thither, and whisked about like a live mouse, turned away with ineffable contempt, saying, "O no, mamma, I don't want that! we've got lots of 'em at home, and don't have to wind 'em up, neither."

No. 173. *Imitation!* — Two children of St. Louis were "playing butcher" not long ago. He who personated the ox doesn't go to school any more. One blow with a hatchet from a sturdy five-year-old, nearly split his head; but he bellowed so frightfully, as to alarm the neighborhood, and bring relief, just as the hatchet was lifted for another blow.

No. 174. *Soliloquies.* — A little six-year-old, while undressing one night, with his arms over his head tying his night-gown behind, was overheard saying to himself, "I can beat Tommy Tucker, I can; I can write my name in writin'; I can tell the time o' day by the clock, I can spell Nebuchadnezzar, yes — and what's more — I can tie a double bow-knot." There's a reasonable amount of self-complacency for you! He was made for an author, and may soon be getting up his autobiography.

No. 175. Another little chap under four,

while wading through a mud-puddle after a heavy shower, came across an angle-worm, and then fell into a reverie,—"Worms — they are the snakes' babies; little mices — they are the rats' babies; and the stars — they are the moon's babies — don't I know"— splash! splash!

No. 176. *Capital definition of Happiness.* — A six-year-old school-girl of Norwich, Connecticut, was asked for a definition of the word "happy." "O, it is to feel as if you wanted to give all your things to your little sister."

No. 177. *A fair Inference.*—"Mamma," said a promising chap of four summers, "if the people are all made of dust, ain't the colored folks made of coal-dust?"

No. 178. *Not so bad.* — A well-known, faithful teacher of Bridgeport, who has charge of an infant class in a Sunday-school there, reports the following case. Not long ago he was talking with them about the origin of Christmas: —

"Where was Christ born?" he asked.

"In Bethlehem."

"Where is Bethlehem?"

"In Judea."

"Who first knew that Christ was born?"

"His mother."

No. 179. *As the Spirit moveth.* — A little Quaker boy, about six years old, after sitting, like the rest of the congregation, in dead silence, all being afraid to speak first, as he thought, got up on the seat, and folding his arms over his breast, murmured, in a sweet, clear voice, just loud enough to be distinctly heard on the fore-seat, "I do wish the Lord would make us all gooder — and gooder — and gooder — till there is no bad left." Would a longer prayer have been more to the purpose?

No. 180. *A Non Sequitur.*—"What have you done with your doll, Amy?" "Lock it up, papa; doin' to teep it for my itty dirl, when I get big, jess like mamma." "Ah, but if you shouldn't have any little girl?" "Never mind, papa — then I'll dive it to my g'*an'chile.*"

No. 181. *A Young Protestant.*—Not long ago, as a crowd of foreigners were presented to the Pope, a little American boy, between four and five years of age, was led up with the rest. The Pope seemed pleased with the bright-eyed little fellow, and lifted his foot somewhat higher than usual, that the boy might more conveniently kiss the cross embroidered upon the toe of his sandal. The boy did not seem to relish the proposition. Drawing himself up, he looked His Holiness full in the face, and said, with emphasis, "*No sir, I won't do it!*" The

Americans and English who were present hardly knew which way to look; but the Pope only smiled good-humoredly, and exclaimed, *Americano!*

The venerable man is said to be "very fond of children, and very indulgent," having none of his own, and no nephews or nieces, *to speak of.*

Not long ago, the little son of an architect employed on certain alterations of St. Peter's Basilica, for a coming festival, was sent by the father to His Holiness, with drawings and specifications. The Pope was so much pleased with the plans, and with the sprightliness of the little messenger, that he led him to a secretary, opened a drawer full of gold pieces, and told him to help himself. "Holy Father," said the little scapegrace, "what if you take 'em and give 'em to me — your hand is bigger than mine." The Pope smiled, and took advantage of the suggestion. So says our "Parisian correspondent."

No. 182. *Another Word for a Blow.*— A little boy and girl were playing on the road-side among the clover-blossoms and butter-cups. The boy, who seemed about five, suddenly took offence, and gave his little playmate, who was still younger, a smart slap on the cheek. She turned away, and sat down in the long grass, and began to cry. At first, the poor boy seemed cross and sulky, as if determined to brave it out, but after a minute or two his beautiful eyes changed color, his mouth trembled, and he said, "I didn't mean to hurt you, Katy, darling — I am sorry." The little rosy face brightened up — the sobs were hushed. "Well, then, if you are sorry," said she, "*it don't hurt me.*"

No. 183. *Just as the Twig is bent, etc. etc.*— In order to amuse the children of a sabbath-school, the teacher began reading to her class the story of David and Goliah; and coming to the passage where Goliah so boastingly dared the stripling shepherd-boy to enter the list, a little chap, newly breeched, up and said to her, "Skip that! skip that! He's blowin'— I want to know who licked."

No. 184. And only yesterday the following illustration of my text happened in Fore-Street. Near Gorham's Corner, two little boys had set themselves in battle-array against a third, somewhat larger. They were all in petticoats, by the way. At last one of the two stepped a little in advance of his companion, and bending his arm like a prize-fighter, sung out, "D'ye see that! jess feel o' that air muscle!" The arm appeared about the size of a turkey's leg, while he was manipulating the biceps; and the countenance that of a trained pugilist. As the bigger boy stepped up to *feel that muscle*, the little fellow let fly, and sent him head over heels into the gutter, petticoats and all.

No. 185. *The Gates Ajar.* — "Our five-year-old," says a neighbor, "stood looking at the new moon a night or two ago. After a long and thoughtful pause, he turned to his mother and whispered, 'Mamma, O mamma! Dod has opened the door a little way.'"

No. 186. *Inferential.* — A mother, who had with her a little daughter, was examining the figure of a horse on a tomb-stone, and wondering what on earth it was an emblem of. There was nothing to explain it, in the inscription. "Mamma," said the little one, as they moved away, "I shouldn't wonder if she died of the *nightmare*."

No. 187. *Capital!*—Just before Washington's birthday, in February last, a teacher, while notifying the class, and preparing them for the holiday, said something to the purpose, about the Father of his Country, and then put the question, —

"Why should we celebrate Washington's birthday any more than *mine?*"

"Because *he never told a lie!*" shouted a young whippersnapper near the door. But as he didn't vanish, probably he didn't mean it. He had only read Weems's "Life of Washington" to advantage, and didn't care who knew it.

No. 188. *Save the Pieces!* — At Winchester, N. H., last winter, a girl of ten, the daughter of O. L. Howard, coasted over a bank twenty feet high, into the Ashuelot river. While on the way she was heard saying to herself, "I'm afraid I shall lose my sled!" But she didn't, and was none the worse for her ducking, though rather damp.

No. 189. *Sublime.* — A cowardly scamp,

though fashionably dressed, having kicked a poor little newsboy, for trying to sell him a paper, the lad hove to, till another boy accosted the "gentleman," and then shouted, in the hearing of all the bystanders, "It's no use to try him, Joe — he can't read."

No. 190. *Constructiveness.* — The Belfast Journal renders an account of a young authoress in that neighborhood, who, at the age of nine, has written the opening chapter of a sensation story. Two of the characters are described as twins, one five, and the other six years old.

No. 191. *Boston Notions.* — The rector of a parish in Toledo, Ohio, was lately catechizing the children of his Sunday-school, and asked, "Where did the wise men come from?" "*From Boston!*" shouted a little wretch, at the top of his voice. Upon further inquiry, it was found that both father and mother were of the Bay-State faith.

No. 192. *Timely Preparation.* — The Lewiston Journal says that a little four-year-old, while standing by her teacher on examination-day, after having spelt cat, dog, ox, cow, and some other monosyllables, suddenly snatched at the teacher's watch-guard, and whispered, "Please, mayn't I be 'smissed after my class gets through readin', so 't I can run home an' get my hair *fizzled* for the 'mittee?" Whereupon the teacher 'smissed her.

No. 193. *Conscience-money.* — A Sunday-school teacher was in the habit of passing round the hat among the little folks, for missionary purposes. One day, he was thrown all aback, on finding a counterfeit shilling among the coppers. Diligent inquiry being had, the little reprobate, who was only expected to give a penny, but an honest penny, was found out. "Georgie," said the teacher, with great seriousness, "didn't you know it was good for nothing?" "To be sure I did," muttered the boy. "Then why did you put it into the box?" "Well, I didn't 'spose the little heathens would know the difference, and so I thought it would be just as good for them."

No. 194. *Combativeness.*—"Look here, mister!" sung out a lad of seven, who had been treed by a ferocious dog; "if you don't call that dog off, I'll eat up all your peaches!"

No. 195. *Childish Faith.*—A little fellow with his first pocket-knife, had it in use most of the time, for several days, occasionally lending it to his playmates, "just to whittle with." One evening, after he had been got ready for the night, and was kneeling by his mother's lap in his night-gown, he finished off the usual service of "Now I lay me," with a "please God give little Jemmy Bailey a knife of his own, so't he won't have to borrow mine all the time."

No. 196. *A Good Lesson for Mothers.*— A bright-eyed, active little fellow, who in due time made his way up to the desk, used to beset his mother, in season and out of season, for a coat like his elder brothers, with pockets behind. To all his importunities, the reply was — "Don't be in a hurry; you are a little boy, — little boys don't wear such coats. When you get to be a man, you shall have a coat with pockets behind." After awhile the boy had to go to the springs for his health; but he shuddered and shrank away from the cold bath. "Why, Charley, you are a man — you shouldn't be afraid."

"O yes, I understand," was the reply; "when I want pockets behind, I am only a little boy; and now that you want me to go in here — *now*, I am a man."

No. 197. *Funeral Ceremonies.* — The San Francisco correspondent of a Sacramento paper tells the following: "A little friend of ours found among the gifts of Santa Claus a plump little waxen-doll. She christened it Maud, and used to take it out for a walk, every pleasant morning. The other day, on seeing a rag of orange-colored merino pinned to a stick by the nursery-door, I peeped in at the children, but was immediately served with notice to quit, by Bobby, who seemed to be the doctor, or a health committee-man; for 'Maud was tooken dreadful bad with the small-pox, and the yeller flag was hung out — didn't I see it?' Soon after this, I heard a piteous wailing, with a sad attempt, and a sadder failure, to sing the sabbath-school hymn, 'Sister thou wast Mild and Lovely,' after which there was a little, crooked, undulating procession, Bobby carrying the dog and Floy the cat, wrapped in shawls, and as they slowly made their way up the hill, into the garden, I understood, from the dismal moaning and sobbing, and from the melancholy rags they bore, that the undertakers were 'performing' a funeral, poor Maud having died of the terrible visitation. I hurried up to the grave, in what I dare say passed for unseemly haste, but just in time to save the poor little wax baby from being buried alive, or, at least, in all her bewitching helplessness. Upon remonstrating, 'We'd ony sowed her up in a bag,' murmured Floy, 'and we would have undigged her.'"

No. 198. *Glimpses of the sabbath-school.* — "Gerty, my dear, you were a very good little girl to-day," said the teacher. "Yes'm — I couldn't help bein good; I got a tiff neck," said Gerty, with perfect seriousness.

"*Who's that a-bearin'?*" — The solemnity of a fashionable church in Chicago was greatly disturbed, not long ago, by a little incident worth remembering. Somebody's three-year-old pet had been often amused at home with pretty good imitations of a bear, growling over his prey. While the congregation were singing, one of those predetermined, zealous worshippers, to be found everywhere, who cannot be persuaded to withhold their contributions in church, though they never dream of pitching a tune anywhere else, began a low, growling accompaniment, within two or three pews of the child, without regard for time or tune, though evidently to his own satisfaction, under an idea that he was singing base — instead of basely. The little one looked surprised, and turning suddenly to mamma, asked, in a voice loud enough to be heard by the whole congregation, just as a lull occurred in the stanza, "O mamma! mamma! who's that *a-bearin'?*"

Will nobody take the hint? Let us have congregational singing by all means, instead of oratorios and operas, for church music — but no menagerie music, if *you* please.

No. 199. *A Plea in Bar.* — "Come up here, you young reprobate, and take a sound spanking," said the teacher, out of all patience with a mischievous, quick-witted boy.

"You ain't got no right to spank me, and the copy you've set for me says so."

"Saucebox! Let me hear you read that copy; read it aloud, so that everybody can hear you."

Whereupon the boy reads, like a trumpet, "'Let all the ends thou aimest at be thy country's!'"

"Go to your seat, you young scapegrace." And he went.

No. 200. *Foresight.* — "Two cocoa-nuts for ten cents! hurrah!" shouted a little shaver to his playfellow across the street; "that'll make me sick to-morrow, and I shan't have to go to school — hurrah!"

No. 201. *I wouldn't, would you?* — A three-year-old youngster saw a drunken fellow staggering through a crowded thoroughfare. "Mother," said he, "did God make that man?" "Yes, my dear." "Well," after considering a moment, "maybe He did, but I wouldn't have done it."

No. 202. *A drop of Gold.* — "Mother," said a little poet of four summers, "just hear the trees makin' music, for the leaves to dance by."

No. 203. *Another!* — A little fellow was eating bread and milk, when he turned round to his mother and exclaimed, "O mother! I'm full of glory! There was a lot o' sunshine in my spoon, and I swallowed it!"

No. 204. *Suggestive.* — "She said she

wouldn't let me go to her funeral, grandma; but you'll let me go to yours, grandma, won't you — there's a dear."

No. 205. *Logical Inference.* — A little boy of our neighborhood, with an eye as clear as a kitten's, had a dog named Caper. Dining with his grandmother not long ago, when they had boiled mutton, his attention was attracted by something he saw in the butter-boat. "What's them, gam'ma?" said he. "Capers, my dear." He looked puzzled — grew thoughtful — and watched the plates awhile, and then, having made up his mind, he came out with, "Please, gam'ma, I want some more o' them little dogs." Of course he had them.

No. 206. *Classification.* — "Who makes the laws of our government?" asked a committee-man of the class under review — a class of Lilliputians. "Congress." "And how is Congress divided?" A dead silence. At last a dear little thing, not more than *so* high, with a wonderful memory, threw up her hand, thereby signifying that she was ready to answer it. "Well," said the teacher, "what say you, Sallie? How are they divided?" "Into civilized, half-civilized, and savage," was the triumphant reply. If it be true, that the greater the truth the greater the libel, might not Miss Sallie be indicted? Congressional miscreants are getting so plentiful, just now, that children should be cautioned — or tongue-tied.

No. 207. *Funny.* — "There now!" said a little bit of a thing, while rummaging a drawer in a bureau, and turning the contents all topsy-turvy, of course; "there now! gran'pa has gone to heaven without his spectacles. Won't you take 'em with you, gramma, when you go?"

No. 208. *A Natural Bonesetter.*—A little fellow pitched head foremost from the top of a coal-bin, and put his shoulder out. A surgeon was sent for "about the quickest." No sooner had the messenger turned his back, than the boy went to work anew, notwithstanding the pain, and while climbing over the back of a chair, as if it were a ladder, he got another tumble, which frightened his poor mother so that she hadn't strength enough to scream. But lo! up jumped the young scapegrace, and began surveying his arm, and shouting, "It's all right, mother! it's all right!" And so it proved. The dislocation had been reduced with a snap, the joint was back in its place, and the young gentleman was ready for another demonstration.

No. 209. *No you don't!*—Freddy, between three and four, and Willie, about five, were both extravagantly fond of milk, and always had a mug of the best, to top off with, at supper; but, being in the country the other day, they happened, for the first time in their lives, to see a girl milking. "There now, Willie," said the youngest, "you see that, don't you? I don't want any more milk after the cow's had it," averting his eyes from the operation as he spoke, with an expression of downright loathing. At supper, when their little mugs of milk were got ready for them, both refused to touch them. On being questioned, Freddy contented himself with saying that, for his part, he didn't want any milk after the cows had it — and there he stopped, as if unwilling to go farther. But Willie came out plump, with an account of the discovery made in the morning.

Their mother saw that she had no time to lose; otherwise an unconquerable repugnance might be associated with their fondness for a wholesome diet, and so she told them how milk was made: that they did not have it from the cows at second-hand, but that when cows ate grass, and clean vegetables, and fruit, they were all changed into milk by a wonderful chemical process, like that which turns all our food to nourishment, giving us flesh and blood, bones and muscle, according to our growth. Willie seemed satisfied with the explanation, and went back to the little mug; but Freddy was not to be persuaded.

After supper Willie took his brother aside into a corner, and was overheard expostulating with him, and saying, "It's all right now, Freddy, and you can go on drinking your milk, just as you always have. The cow eats grass, and that's what makes it. Now if the cow didn't eat the grass, you'd have to, you see. That's what the cow's for."

Freddy went back to his milk without another word, as being, at the worst, somewhat more agreeable than eating grass.

No. 210. *Little Pitchers have Big Ears.*—A child, the son of a minister, sat on the floor playing with his blocks one afternoon, when two or three female parishioners dropped in for a dish of chat with mamma. The conversation, after a few moments, turned, very naturally, it may be supposed, on a floating scandal of the day. They had entirely forgotten the child; but all at once recollected themselves, and came to a sudden stop, and, looking at each other, tried to recall what had been said.

There sat the little imp, busy with his playthings, and, as it appeared upon further inquiry, after the visitors had gone, without having understood a syllable of what had been said; but the lively chattering stopped so suddenly, he looked up, and then, turning over and rolling on the floor, as if unable to restrain himself, he sung out, "Go on! go right on! that's jess sech as I like to hear, every day!"

No. 211. *A Hint for the Doctor.* — A little four-year-old midget being in a bad way, was called upon to take a very nauseous medicine, and was sitting in a high chair, in her night-dress, when the cup was offered her. She shook her head with a piteous look, and then said, "No no — me tan't tate it so; but me'll tate it with soogar," and sent off the nurse for a lump. Whereupon her little brother rushed up to her, shouting, "Take it, Sallie! take it, while she's gone, Sallie, and cheat her! and then hide, Sallie — that's the way I do." And thereupon Miss Sallie gulped down the abominable mixture to the last dregs, without winking, only saying, "It choke Sallie," and then scrabbling down from the high chair, and scuttling away under the bed, with an occasional chuckle, and popping out her little curly head, her eyes dancing with joy, while waiting for the nurse to get back. When she appeared, she was welcomed with a shout of triumph by the youthful conspirators, Miss Sallie never dreaming for a moment that she had been bamboozled.

No. 212. *The best of Reasons.* — "Breakfasting with a physician the other day," says somebody, whose name does not appear in the record, "little Julia began to talk very earnestly, at the first pause in the conversation. Her father checked her, somewhat sharply, saying, 'Why is it that you always talk so much?' ' 'Tause I've dot somesin to say,' was the reply. The solemn papa was obliged to look another way, while the guests laughed outright."

No. 213. *Discouraging.* — A little boy named Knight, of the mission-school at New-London, was told by the teachers, one and all, that if he was good, he would go to heaven. The little fellow accepted the situation, and evidently did his best; but the next time he appeared in his place, he seemed down-hearted. On being questioned by his teacher about the cause, and asked if he had been a good boy, he replied, "Yes — I've tried ever so hard to be good; but it's no use. The boys tell me I can't go to heaven, if I am ever so good." "And why not, pray?" "Because they tell me the Bible says there'll be no *Knight* there."

No. 214. *How to fix it.* — Master Willie, a very good boy, as boys go, happened to begin going to school, just when the first snow fell, and a pretty new sled, with scarlet runners, had become his property. About school-time, therefore, he began to have *such* terrible aches. But these would soon pass off, and then he would go off to slide. One morning he came to his mamma with a *drefful* headache — and school had to be given up. "Very well, my dear," said she; "if you have such a terrible headache, you can stay at home this beautiful morning; but remember, you mustn't ask leave to go and slide, for I shall not consent — I tell you now." "Yes, mamma." But within the next half hour Willie came to her, saying his drefful headache was all gone, and would she let him go just this once. "No, Willie — you know what I said — you wouldn't have me tell a lie, would you?"

Willie turned away somewhat discouraged; but after a few moments his little face brightened up, as with inward sunshine, and he stole up to his mother's knee, and whispered, — "No, mother! No, no! I don't want you to tell a lie; but couldn't you *just fix it*, you see, as you do when you put me to bed, and say you are not going out, and then go?"

No. 215. *Excuse my Candor.*—"What a fine head your little boy has!" said a propitiatory friend—a phrenologist, perhaps—to a doating father. "Ay, ay," said the delighted papa; "ay, ay, he's a chip of the old block, ain't you, sonny?" "I guess so," said the boy, "for teacher says I'm a little blockhead."

No. 216. *One of the Upper Ten.*—"Ma," said a little moppet, "if I should die and go to heaven, would I wear my moire antique?" "No, darling, we cannot suppose we shall carry the fashions of this world into the next." "Then, Ma, how would the little angels know I belonged to the best society?"

No. 217. *Catching the Idea.*—A little chap, on his return from church, one day, where he heard an organ for the first time in his life, said to his mother, "O, mammy, how I do wish you had been at church to-day, to see the fun. There was a man there pumping music out of an old cupboard."

No. 218. *Rather embarrassing.*—A young lady — all women are ladies, you know — wishing to impress upon her class in the sabbath-school the terrible effect of Nebuchadnezzar's punishment, assured them that for seven long years he ate grass *like a cow.* Up jumped a little boy with, "Please, ma'am, did he give milk?" It is said the answer was not forthcoming.

No. 219. *Total Depravity again.*—"O sister! sister!" said little Mattie, "if you would only let me swear once — only just once!" her heart being too full for utterance.

No. 220. *A timely Suggestion.*—Mamma was telling Master Freddy about the sacrifice, or intended sacrifice, of Isaac, and explaining the illustration which appeared in the old family Bible. There lay the boy, bound hand and foot, on the altar, with the faggots heaped about him, and the great sacrificial knife just ready to descend, and almost touching the nose of the ram. She was explaining, to the best of her knowledge and belief, the necessity of the sacrifice, and the providential appearance of the substitute, when Freddy, whose feelings had been worked up to concert pitch, exclaimed, "Sheepy, sheepy! why don't you grab the knife, and run?"

No. 221. *Tenderness of Conscience.* — "Dad — I say, dad — Nathan swored last first-day, I heard him," said the little son of Master Blair, a Scotch Quaker, I once knew. "Ah — an' what deed he say, mon?" "He said Old Scratch, an' I heard him."

No. 222. *Beautiful — exceedingly!* — A

little one was talking about home. "And where is your home, dear?" said a listener. Looking up into his mother's face with loving eyes, he whispered, "*Where mother is.*"

No. 223. *An embryo Metaphysician.* — "What are you going to see, Sherwood?"

"Nothing, gran'pa."

"Nothing, my boy — how can you see nothing?"

"Easy enough, gran'pa."

"Where would you look for it?"

"Down a well, gran'pa."

"Isn't there something burning here?" said the mother of this boy one day, on coming into the room where he was at play, and sniffing as she spoke.

"Yes, mamma," sniffing in reply.

"Bless me — what is it?"

"Coal, mamma."

No. 224. *Influence of Example.* — The

little son of a friend in the army, had learned to curse heartily, whenever anything disturbed him; his father, of whom he had caught the trick, was ordered off, not long ago, to a distant part of the country. Being separated from his boy, and having had time for reflection, perhaps, he wrote home to his wife that he was sorry to hear how little Joe still continued to curse and swear. "Who told him?" said the boy. "He says a little bird told him," was the mother's reply. "D—n that bird!" exclaimed the little scapegrace. He was only six. While yet a baby, but just able to make himself understood, an Irish girl came rushing in to the mother one day, saying, "O ma'am! he keeps a-sayin' Jesus Christ, in the barn!"

No. 225. *Retribution.* — "Tell you what 'tis, I won't pray for you when I say my prayers, Willie," said a little thing to her playfellow in the next house; "and Jesus won't bless you, *and*" — after a little hesitation — " *and* — He shan't redeem you, neither !"

No. 226. *A young Poet.* — A little four-year-old, laboring to impress a sister with the prodigious quantity of something he had promised to give her, said, "You just turn the sky over and I'll fill it full — chock-full."

No. 227. *Literalness.* — "*I* know!" said a little boy to whom his mother was reading that passage where the Lord is said to be walking in the garden in the cool of the day; " I know! Just as papa does, with his hands behind him, and an old coat on."

No. 228. *Letting the delicious Secret out.* — Soon after his mother's second marriage, a little shaver reached out his hand for another piece of sponge-cake. Step-father shakes his head, and says *No*, after a fashion that seems to admit of no appeal. "Well," says the boy, "I don't care — only we're sorry we ever married you;" and then, as if concentrating all the bitterness he felt, in a withering outburst, he added, "And mother says so too!"

No. 229. *Their Notions of another World.* "Well then," said a little girl, throwing down her book, "I don't want to die and go to heaven that way; but if God would just let down a big basket, and draw me up with a rope, I do think I should like it."

No. 230. Another little girl, after being made to understand what a *post mortem* examination was, declared that she would never consent to be so dealt with, after death.

"What! when it would be such a help to the living, my dear?"

"Fiddle-de-dee! how would I look going to heaven all cut to pieces?"

No. 231. *Another.* — Lottie, lying sick with a fever, having lost a dear little cousin not long before, was unwilling to take her medicine, till she was promised a pair of ear-rings. By and by, when she was believed to be sound asleep, her mother was suddenly startled by a burst of loud laughter. Being asked what was the matter, Lottie said, "O, it tickles me so to think how cousin Hiram *will* laugh, when he sees me come trottin' into heaven with my new ear-rings!"

No. 232. *A Justification.* — "Golly! — Gosh! — Gracious!" shouted a funny little chap, at something he saw.

"Why, Bobby," said his mother, "where *did* you pick up such words?"

"O, I've heard *you* say Gracious, mamma, and the golly-gosh I just made up myself," was the reply.

One day this dear mother, who had expostulated and pleaded with him till she had no patience left, said she could bear with him no longer; she wouldn't have a little boy round her that used such language; and so she would have to put him away, and try to find another little son. In the bitterness and desolation of his heart, Master Bobby went out into the yard, and sat down on the grass to have a good cry by himself; whereupon a little bantam rooster, not understanding the case, flew up on the fence, and fell a-crowing like all possessed. "Shut up, darn you!" blubbered Bobby, through his big dropping tears; "I've trouble enough on my mind, without you!" He had just promised never to use that, nor any other naughty word again, while he breathed the breath of life.

And for a time he kept his promise. But one day, just when they began to feel greatly encouraged, he burst into the room with, "Oh, mother! what do you think? I was coming through the field just now, and a horse was tied there — the wickedest horse ever you *did* see; an' he jist stood still there, and kept sayin' 'By golly!' and 'By gosh!' and 'Dod darn you!' and everything else he could think of. If you'd a been there, you'd a-whipped him, oh, ever so hard, mamma! wouldn't you? And so would I, if I'd had a whip." His mind was relieved.

No. 233. *Fishing and Mousing.* — "Some years ago," says the New England correspondent of — I forget what paper, "my cousin kept a district school. Among her scholars was a little fellow of perhaps four years of age, but too young to speak plainly. One day, when all the others were hard at work, this youngster got hold of a pin and a string. The pin he bent into the shape of a fish-hook, baiting it with a morsel of cheese. He had seen a mouse come up through a hole in the corner of the hearth, not long before, and went to work 'bobbing for whales.' On being asked what he was at, he answered, 'Fishin' for a mousie.' This being rather out of the usual course of study, the teacher, by way of punishment, ordered him to stay where he was, and keep bobbing, till further orders. After a while, there was a commotion; the mouse, it seemed, had swallowed the cheese, hook and all, and the next moment Master Jerry, giving a sudden jerk, sprang into the middle of the room, and swinging the mouse round his head, shouted, 'I've dut 'im! I thware I've dut 'im!'"

No. 234. *Sunday-school Conundrums.* — A smart little chap, with a wicked eye, on being asked what was the chief end of man, replied, "The end what's got the head on."

No. 235. *Inferential.* — "Oh, mamma! mamma!" shouted a little shaver, as he saw the sun going down, all red, like the opening to a furnace-fire, "see how hot the sky is over there! Santa Claus is bakin', I guess."

Another of these natural philosophers, in petticoats, on hearing a man dump coal into the bin with a terrible rumbling, shouted, "Oh, mother! now I know what makes thunder. It is God puttin' coal on."

No. 236. *Coming to the Point.* — "Tilly, my love," said a young mother to a daughter in her fourth summer, "what would you do without your mother?"

"I should put on every day just such a dress as I wanted to," said Tilly, coquetting with her little fan.

No. 237. *Second Thoughts.* — "O papa, is it wrong to change your mind?" "Well, no, my boy — that depends upon circumstances; but why do you ask?" "You know I wanted to be a doctor, papa," said the little five-year-old. "O yes, I remember; and what then?" "Well, if you please, papa, I'd rather be a candy-store."

No. 238. *Special Pleading.* — "A friend at Lewiston," says one of our newspapers, "told his little Josey, about six years of age, not to go out of the gate again without leave. Soon after, papa missed him from the back-yard, and saw him a long way off, tumbling about on the sidewalk. He went after him, and taking him by the hand, leading him toward the house, and considering the question of punishment for such disobedience, he asked him why he left the yard, when he had been told not to do so. 'Well, you see, papa, you told me not to go out o' the gate; but you didn't tell me not to climb over the fence.'" Demurrer sustained. — Plea adjudged good, and no *respondeas ouster* allowed.

No. 239. *And why not?* — "Lottie," said a little visitor, "what makes your Kitty so cross?" "Oh, tause she's tuttin' her teef, I 'spec."

No. 240. *Vagabondizing.* — Two Illinois chaps, one twelve, and the other only eight, left their homes not long ago to see the world, or seek their fortunes, without money or friends, and journeyed away off into Iowa, three hundred miles or so. The father of one, after snuffing about for two or three days, got upon their track, and followed them to Rock-Grove, Iowa, where he found them pretty well used up, though far from being sick of their bargain. They had no explanations to give — no excuses to offer — but, so far as could be discovered, had no reason for leaving their homes, or running away; and they had actually travelled the whole distance, on railroads and stages, without money and without price.

No. 241. *Strange — if true.* — "Harry!

you shouldn't throw away nice bread like that; you may want it yourself before you die." "Well, mother, and if I should, would I stand any better chance of getting it then, if I should eat it now?"

No. 242. *Am I dead, Papa?* — Many a child has propounded that same question, with all seriousness, after a narrow escape. The first words of a little boy who had just been fished up at New London lately, were — "*Be I dead, though?*"

No. 243. *Enlisted for the War.* — A little three-year-old, whose father, a clergyman, had presented him with a military cap, all "fuss and feathers," insisted on wearing it everywhere, and at all times, marching through all the rooms, to music of his own, hour after hour, and day after day, until his mother found it worth her while to remind him that soldiers didn't train on the Sabbath.

Whereupon, our young gentleman started off up stairs, left foot first, with a new tune, compounded of Hail-Columbia and Yankee-Doodle, Mother-Goose and Bobbylink, saying, as he held on his way, — *"But I'm a soldier of the Lord, mamma."*

No. 244. *Repeating the Colic.* — The rector of an Episcopal Church in Albany, who had taken the greatest pains with his sabbath-school, and prided himself not a little on the proficiency of his scholars, called upon them one day, after a whole week of preparation, to repeat the *Collect*. A dead silence: then for a show of hands; not a hand was lifted; but, on casting his eyes over the little community, he saw a sign of encouragement. "Ah, ha!" said he, "I see a little hand raised in Miss Annie's class. Please repeat the *Collect*, my dear." The poor thing seemed bewildered. "If you know the Collect, Fanny," said the teacher, "why don't you repeat it?" The child blushed and stammered; but on being further questioned, said, "I thought he wanted all that had the *colic* to hold up their hands; and I had it t'other night, and father had to stay up, and take care of me." To *repeat* her *colic* would be no joke to her, whatever it might be to others, and she was probably excused.

No. 245. *Instinctive Perception.* — How wonderful that children so rarely misapply uncommon words, even where they do not understand them — being their own interpreters. A boy of nearly fourteen, was fishing for trout in a deep, clear brook. A stout, lubberly negro began teasing him, and throwing mud at him. The boy jumped up, and swinging the fish-pole round his head with all his might, fetched the colored gemman such a wipe with the butt, as to send him headlong into the water — where he left him floundering — and cleared out. When he reached home, on being called upon by his mother for an explanation of his uncomfortable appearance, he told her how it had happened. The mother was indignant: to have her boy so treated by a nigger was too much. "And did you brook the outrage?" she asked. "No mother," said the boy, catching the idea, though he did not quite understand the word, "no mother, *but I brooked the nigger.*"

No. 246. *A puzzling Question.* — A minister of the Gospel, while preparing a discourse for the following Sabbath, stopped now and then to review what he had written, to alter and erase here and there. "Father," said a young theologian of about five, just entering upon the ministry, "father, does God tell you what to preach?" "Certainly, my child." "Then what makes you scratch it out?"

No. 247. *Let Brotherly Love prevail.*— Another of like spirit, under five, in his regular evening prayer, remembered his younger brother with a sob, who was in a very bad way, after the following fashion: "Oh Lord, don't let my little brother die. Help Dr. S., oh Lord, to make him well — though his parents *are* Democrats."

No. 248. *Baby Champions.* — In the "Life of Aaron Burr," by Davis, we have a little incident — the first — which that bad man delighted to recall. An old he-goat, or a ram, I forget which, came at his little grandson, while yet a baby, and threatened him with his horns. The child, having the blood of his grandfather in him, seized a stick, and let him have it with such effect, that the animal sheered off, greatly to the satisfaction of "grumpa," who saw it from the window. And here is another case *in pint.* A little four-year-old of Mr. Cheney, living in Ashland, N. H., was playing on the front yard with a younger sister and a pet bantam. A large hawk suddenly swooped down upon the poor thing, fastened his talons upon it, and would have carried it off but for the child, who, seizing a hatchet he had been playing with, fell upon the hawk, and pounded him till he let go his prey, and "skedaddled."

No. 249. *Budding Nature.* — Matthews used to tell a story about a little boy, who, on seeing the cherubim sculptured in Westminster-Abbey, exclaimed, "O mamma, how I do wish I was a cherubim!" to the great joy of his mother, who had to spank him oftener than he thought desirable; but, on being asked wherefore, he said — almost sobbing — "'Cause they ain't got nothin' but wings and head," rubbing his — behind — at the same time, with uncommon energy.

"Ah," said another little chap to a playfellow who had just been sorely trounced, "Ah, ha! I guess you hain't got any gran'-mother!"

And again. "Mamma," said another little tantrybogus, "why are them orphans you talk so much about, and pity so much, the happiest little creatures in the world, arter all?" "They are not, my son; but why do you ask?" "'Cause they hain't got nobody to wallop 'em."

No. 250. *A definition of Pride.*—"What is *pride*, my dear?" "Walking with a cane, when you ain't lame," said the little four-year-old to whom the query was propounded.

No. 251. *Liberty of Speech.*—"Chickerin', is meetin' out?" said a little fellow, perched upon a high fence, many years ago, to Dr. Chickering, on his way from church.

No. 252. The same little rogue, who, by

the way, has gone bravely up since, leaving his own monument behind him — as most people do, I believe — was crowing pretty loudly one day, when I was going by. "Holloa there!" said I, "Holloa! I can lick you, Sam Fessenden!"

"Well — I'll tell you what you can't do!" said he.

"What is it?"

"You can't give me a rockin'-horse."

No. 253. *Admirable Definition.* — At one of the ragged schools of Ireland, a clergyman asked, "What is holiness?"

A dirty, ragged little wretch jumped up, and sung out, "Plase your riverence, it's bein clane inside."

No. 254. *Another.* — A boy, eight years old, having been told that a reptile is an animal that creeps, and being asked on examination-day to name one, answered, without winking, "*A baby.*"

No. 255. *A Young Butcher.* — A boy in New York, only five years old, having heard papa say that he wished the two calves they had in the barn were killed, got a hammer, and going to the barn by himself, succeeded in killing them both; and returned to the house to tell the story — to report progress and ask leave to sit again, as we say at Washington, after a similar feat.

No. 256. *Flat Contradiction.* — "What's that?" said a school-master, pointing to the letter X. "It's daddy's name," said the boy. "No, you little blockhead, it's X." "Tain't X, neither," said the boy; "it's daddy's name, for I seed him write it many a time."

No. 257. *A delicate Scruple.* — "Oh, mamma!" said a little chap, the other day, who had been listening to her conversation with a neighboring gossip; "did you say I was born a-Sunday?"

"Yes, my child."

"Ain't I wicked, mamma?"

"Why, what makes you ask such a question, Bobby?"

"Well, ain't I a sabbath-breaker, for bein born a-Sunday? But, mamma, I didn't mean to — I'm sure I didn't."

No. 258. *A desirable Parentage.* — A crowd of dirty, ragged little creatures were loitering about the large show-window of a confectionery-shop. "O my! don't I wish he was my father!" said a little barefooted girl, with her fist in her mouth. Was her sincerity to be doubted?

No. 259. *Not to be mealy-mouthed.* — "I dare say when you get back to mamma, Charlie, my boy, she'll have a nice present for you. What would you like best, Charlie? a little brother, or a little sister?" "Well now, Uncle George," after considering awhile, "if it makes no difference to Ma, I'd rather have a pony."

No. 260. *High-school Training.*—"I say, Ma! do you know what the pyro — pyro — pyrotechnical remedy is, for a crying baby?" said a little miss of thirteen, with cherry lips and roguish eyes.

"Gracious goodness me! no; I never heard of such a thing."

"Well, ma — it's *rock-it!*"

No. 261. *School Exercises.* — "Well, Maggie, what do they do at school?" "They whips me." "And then what do you do?" "I tingle, skeam, and dance." Another group of three were questioned. The oldest said, "He had to get grammar, arithmetic, geography," etc., etc. The second, that he "got readin', spellin', and *diffinitions.*" "And what do you get my little man?"— to Master Jack, who happened just then to be spearing the cat with a wooden sword. "Oh, I gets lots — I gets readin', and spellin', and spankin'; and then I gets up in the mornin' — sometimes."

No. 262. *Childish Inferences.* — "Come now, children, speak up! What is it that makes the sea, salt?" "Codfish!" screamed a boy from a distant corner of the room; "Codfish!" as if he were crying the article to a Down-East population, Saturday morning.

No. 263. *Great Forbearance.* — "O, Ma," said a little creature, who had been allowed to stay at communion for the first time, "what do you think! a man went round with a plateful of money, and offered it to everybody in our pew; but I didn't take any."

No. 264. *A gentle rebuke for the Earl of—,* a pompous and niggardly gentleman, who personally superintends the dairy where he lives, and actually sells the milk to the children with his own hands.

One morning, a pretty child, standing a-tiptoe, with her pitcher and penny held up, caught the eyes of this nobleman. "Now," said he, "my pretty lass — *now*," patting her on the head, and giving her a kiss — "*now*, you may tell, as long as you live, that you have been kissed by an Earl."

"O yes — but you took the penny, though," said the little witch, innocently enough, I dare say. But what became of the Earl? Nobody knows. It was a long while ago.

No. 265. *Where do all the Cooks go?* — A capital housekeeper having discharged her cook with emphasis, exclaimed, "Well, thank heaven! there are no cooks in the other world." Which other world did she mean, think you? Her little girl seemed puzzled; but, after thinking awhile, said, "Well, mamma, then who cooks wash-days? for you know they must have a big wash, as they always wear white."

No. 266. *More Sabbath-school Exercises.* — "Where was John Rogers burned? — tell me now," said a teacher, in a voice that filled the room, and startled the listeners at the door. "Couldn't tell," said the first. No answer from the next. "Joshua knows," whispered a little thing at the head of her class. "Well, then, if Joshua knows, he may tell," said the teacher. "In the fire," shouted Joshua, with a look of imperturbable self-complacency.

No. 267. *Just as the twig is bent, etc., etc.* — A little shaver, living in Walcott, Maine, aged only five years, having well considered the subject of earning his bread, went to a farmer and offered his services. He was put to raking hay, and persevered as long as the rest, and went home to his happy mother in the evening, with a silver dollar in his pocket. And where did he get it? some lazy little Jackanapes will ask, I dare say. Go to your mother, child.

No. 268. *Them's my Sentiments.*—A six-year-old boy was set to work upon what is called a "composition," all about water. He wrote as follows: "Water is good to drink. Water is good to paddle in and swim in, and to skate on when it grows hard in winter. When I was a little wee baby, nurse used to wash me every morning in cold water — *ugh!* I have heard tell the Injuns only wash themselves once in ten years. I wish I was an Injun."

No. 269. *Arithmetic made easy.*—"Peter—I say, Peter! what are you doing with that boy?" "Helping him in 'rethmetic, sir." "How helping him?" "He wanted to know if I took ten from seventeen, how many would be left; and so I took ten of his apples to show him, an' now he wants 'em back."

"And why don't you give 'em back, hey?"

"'Cause I want him to remember how many was left."

No. 270. *Scripture and Poetry.* — While a poor mother was moaning over her wretchedness and helplessness, fearing that she would have to go to the workhouse, her little boy looked up from his pile of blocks in the chimney-corner, and murmured, "Mamma, I think God hears, when we scrape the bottom of the barrel."

No. 271. *A glorious Boy.* — The playmates of a small boy were trying to persuade him to take a handful or two of cool, ripe cherries, from a tree overhanging the stonewall, where they were sitting together in the hot sunshine.

"What are you afeard of?" said the largest, "for if your father should find it out, he is so kind, he wouldn't punish you."

"That's the very reason why I wouldn't touch 'em," said the dear little fellow, in reply.

No. 272. *Physics and Metaphysics.* — An

amiable professor, in France, was laboring to explain that theory, according to which the body is entirely renewed every six years, giving for illustration the experiment made with a pig, by feeding it on madder till its bones were colored through and through, and other cases. "And so, mam'selle," said he, addressing a pretty little blonde with a roguish face, "in six years you will be no longer Mademoiselle F——."

"I hope so," murmured Mam'selle F., casting down her eyes, and peering up at him through her long lashes. Evidently she had somewhat misunderstood her teacher.

No. 273. *Too good to be true.* — A little boy having broken his rocking-horse the very day it was brought home, his mother began scolding him. "Why, mamma," said he, with a mischievous giggle, as if he understood the joke, and *meant* it, "What's the use of a horse afore he's *broke?*"

No. 274. *True, beyond all question.* — Said somebody to a little moppet, as she sat on the door-step playing with her kitten and her doll, "Which do you love best, darling, your kitten or your doll?"

After looking serious for a minute or two, she leaned over and whispered, "I love Kitty best, but please don't tell Dolly."

No. 275. *A slight Misapprehension.* — Three little negroes were lately baptized by our friend, Mr. C., of the new Protestant Cathedral. After the ceremony was over, one of them whispered to its mother, "You don't mind it, mamma, do you, 'cause he baptized us in his night-gown?"

No. 276. *A Natural Curiosity.* — A dear little six-year-old was going by a church with her father. "What house is that?" asked the child. "That is the Dutch Church," said papa; "people go there to be good, so

that, after a while, they may be angels."
"Hi! then there'll be Dutch angels, papa!"

No. 277. *Much to the Point.* — A sabbath-school teacher had been reading to her class the beautiful story of Ruth — with a running accompaniment. Wishing to call their attention to the kindness of the princely husbandman, in ordering the reapers to drop here and there a handful of wheat, she said, "Now, children, Boaz did another nice thing for poor Ruth: can you tell me what it was?"

"To be sure I can," said a little fellow, a long way off; — "*he married her.*"

No. 278. *A new Currency.* — Our Sallie, a pleasant, active, sprightly little thing, just old enough to make herself understood, partly by pantomime and partly by lisping, came in all of a glow, saying, —

"O mamma! mamma! Me jess buyed a itte paper-doll."

"Indeed! and where did you buy it?"

"O, jess down here, in a defful big store; me toot a ittle dirl in me's hand."

"And where did you get your money to pay for it?"

"O, me didn't buy it for money, mamma — me jess gived the gemman a fower to pay for it."

And sure enough! Upon further inquiry, it turned out that the little midget had entered a large store, made her way into the back part — one of the largest establishments in Brooklyn, by the way — and seeing some paper-dolls in hand, wanted to buy one; but having no money, offered a flower she had just gathered on the way, which the shopman received with all seriousness, regarding it as a lawful tender.

No. 279. *A new handle for Pussy.* — Little three-year-old Mary was playing roughly with her pet kitten. After pulling its ears, she began carrying it by the tail. "Baby, dear," said her mother, "you hurt pussy." "No I don't, mamma — 'cause I'm carryin' it by the handle."

No. 280. *A new Puzzle.* — A pretty little thing under five, on being questioned by her mother about her Bible lesson, was asked, among other matters, why the Lord wouldn't let Adam and his wife eat of the forbidden fruit; and answered, that she "didn't know for certain, but rather thought, maybe He wanted to can it for his own use."

No. 281. *More Logic.* — In our Putnam for October, there are two charming little manifestations of boyish character and boyish reasoning. A chap of only five, soon after the fire at Barnum's Museum, which he had investigated, was very anxious to know if there really were any such creatures as devils, "with horns, hoofs, bats'-wings and eagles' claws"—he had just been looking at an illustrated Pilgrim's Progress. Mamma tried to put him off, but in vain. At last, he broke out with, "Well—I don't believe there is any, for Barnum would be sure to have one." And then, after another glance at the illustration, he added, "How funny he *would* look in a cage, with his horns and tail!"

The same little fellow hid his face in his mother's lap one day, while it thundered. To soothe him, his mother explained the phenomena of thunder and lightning. A lull followed, and he ran off to play in a distant corner of the room. Then followed another burst, louder than usual. Back he ran to his mother, exclaiming, "I don't see what fun 'tis for God to go thunderin' round so!" Of course not.

No. 282. *Natural History.*—According to Peter Pindar, Sir Joseph Banks' fleas were lobsters till he boiled them, when "d—d a one turned red;" whereat he exclaimed, according to the same authority, who, in his own mortal extremity, if Byron may be credited, —

———— "Supprest
With a death-bed sensation a blasphemous jest,"

"Fleas are *not* lobsters — d—n their souls!"

But another question has lately come up. A little girl, of the Buffalo tribe, wants to know if fleas are *white;* "cauth untle teld her that Mary had a little lamb with *fleas* as white as snow."

Another. — A charity scholar — perhaps one of the Ragged School — on being asked, after an examination in the Psalms, "What was the Pestilence that walketh in darkness?" answered,—"Bed bugth, thir!"— Not so much out of the way, after all; since fleas only *hop* in darkness.

No. 283. *Cross-examination.* — Says a neighbor, "Wife was undressing a little four-year-old — Charley — the other evening. After he was set free, he began to feel of his fat, chubby arms, with manifest self-complacency; and looking up into his mother's face, he said, 'Mamma, who made me?'"

"'The Good Man away up in the sky,'" said mamma.

"Whereupon Charley grew thoughtful, and after looking up through the tree-tops into the clear blue starlit sky for a few minutes, added, 'But, mamma, who took me down?'"

No. 284. *A Broad Hint.* — There was an aged country clergyman, who found so little time for study, that when fairly at work, he wouldn't allow his grandchildren to romp in the passage, or play hide-and-seek, or leap-frog in the study — the monster!

"Ma," said one of these little fellows, who

had been snubbed for riotous behavior one day, "I say, Ma,"—she had just been telling him about heaven—"I say, Ma, I don't want to go to heaven." "Don't want to go to heaven, Georgie!" "No, Ma, I'm sure I don't." "And why not?" "Why, gran'pa will be there, won't he?" "Why yes—I hope so." "Well—jest as soon as he sees us, he'll come scoldin' along, and say,—'Whew—whew—whew! What are these boys here for?'"

No. 285. *Patronage.* — "I say, dad—have you ben to the Museum yet?" said a young American of ten. "No, my son." "Well, jest you go, and mention my name to the door-keeper, an' he'll take you round and show you everything."

No. 286. *Childish Cunning.* — "A child who is good at excuses is seldom good for anything else," quoth Franklin. A naughty little chap, says a cotemporary, went blubbering into the backyard, because his mother wouldn't allow him to go down to the river on the Sabbath. On being further remonstrated with, he said, "But, mamma, I didn't want to go in a-swimmin' with 'em; I only wanted to go down an' see the bad little boys drown, for goin' in a-swimmin' on a Sunday — boo-hoo, boo-hoo!"

No. 287. *Childish Trust.* — The following illustration of the passage, "Whosoever shall not receive the Kingdom of God as a little child, he shall not enter therein," will, I am sure, be thankfully received.

As the train stopped, a gentleman who had been seriously engaged in conversation with another, who had a little boy with him, said to the child, after bidding the father farewell— "Good-by, Charley; take care of yourself."

"My father will take care of me," said the boy, with a look of unquestioning trust.

No. 288. *What shall we pray for?*—A child of seven had been packed to bed quite early for something rather serious. At the usual hour of bedtime, her mother sat down by the bedside to read prayers for the day. "Mamma," said the little one, "please read the prayer for persons in affliction."

No. 289. *A Poser.*—"Well then—who took care of the babies?" asked a little girl, on hearing her mother say that all people were once children.

No. 290. *Another Poser.*—Aunt Bessie had been laboring with Master Jack, to persuade him to go to bed at set of sun; urging for his consideration that the dear little chickens always went to roost at that time. "Yes, auntie—I know that—but then the old hen always goes with 'em!"

No. 291. *A reasonable Being.*—"Halloa, mamma! halloa there!" shouted the angel of the household, from the top of the garret stairs, "I'm mad as fire — and Hannah won't pacify me."

No. 292. *Mind your Pronunciation.* — A gentlewoman of Belfast, Ireland, was questioning a child in a charity school, about what the wife of a king, and the wife of an emperor were called; and then she added for their encouragement, "And now what is the wife of a duke called?"—"A drake! a drake!" shouted half a dozen little voices.

No 293. *Foresight, Sagacity, and Thrift.*— Little Master Jemmy began to save the change that fell in his way at a very early age, in the hope of being a rich man, like Messrs A., B., and C., who rode in their carriages, or "swung on the gate" all day long, with "a *little more* fat pork," after their wishes had been granted for "as *much fat pork as they could eat.*"

One morning, at breakfast, when he was

about gobbling the last mouthful, his aunt informed him, that during the night a pair of babies had been added to the family, already consisting of three beside Jemmy.

The boy dropped his knife and fork, and sung out, — "Good gracious, Aunt Mary! if father and mother keep on at this rate, there won't be fifty dollars a-piece for us!"

www.ingramcontent.com/pod-product-compliance
Lightning Source LLC
Chambersburg PA
CBHW031956230426
43672CB00010B/2174